ƒP

STREET
FIGHTER
MARKETING
SOLUTIONS

**How One-On-One Marketing Will
Help You Overcome the Sales Challenges
of Modern-Day Business**

JEFF SLUTSKY

FREE PRESS

New York London Toronto Sydney

*f*P

FREE PRESS
A Division of Simon & Schuster, Inc.
1230 Avenue of the Americas
New York, NY 10020

FREE PRESS and colophon are trademarks of Simon & Schuster, Inc.

For information about special discounts for bulk purchases,
please contact Simon & Schuster Special Sales:
1-800-456-6798 or business@simonandschuster.com.

STREETFIGHTER is a registered trademark of Streetfighter Marketing, Inc.

Designed by Nancy Singer Olaguera / ISPN Publishing Services

Manufactured in the United States of America

10   9   8   7   6   5   4   3   2   1

Library of Congress Cataloging-in-Publication Data
Slutsky, Jeff.
   Street fighter marketing solutions: How one-on-one marketing will help
   you overcome the sales challenges of modern-day business / Jeff Slutsky.
   —1st Free Press hardcover ed.
       p. cm.
   1. Marketing—Management. 2. Sales promotion. 3. Advertising.
     I. Title.
   HF5415.13.S593 2007
   658.8—dc22   2007005121

ISBN-13: 978-0-7432-9914-5
ISBN-10:   0-7432-9914-0

Dedication

To my wife, Helene, the perfect woman for me

CONTENTS

STREET

FIGHTER

MARKETING

SOLUTIONS

HOW THIS BOOK HELPS YOUR BUSINESS

It must sometimes seem like you are being hit from every side; whether it's big-box retailers, internet competition, skyrocketing overhead, or a glut of competing businesses, the pressures push you up against the wall. What you desperately need is a war chest of proven ideas, strategies, and tactics that will help your business not only survive but really prosper! That is what *Street Fighter Marketing Solutions* is all about.

In the current hypercompetitive, advertising-polluted environment, you pay more and get less for your marketing dollar, which means that it costs you more to attract customers than ever before. Yet you are likely putting the majority of your marketing dollars into some form of local mass advertising. You might use your daily newspaper or other print media; local broadcast or cable television; radio; billboards or other outdoor media; and, most likely, you're in the yellow pages. Each one of these traditional advertising media has suffered an erosion of its effectiveness. This downward trend coupled with the ever-increasing proliferation of marketing choices is likely to continue.

Realizing that your local mass media has lost some of its

muscle, you've probably experimented with other forms of marketing, such as the internet, direct mail, telemarketing, sponsorships, local neighborhood marketing, event promotions, PR, and even handing out pens, coffee cups, T-shirts, and can cozies with your logo on them. Despite all this investment in your marketing, you've probably not been happy with your results.

There is a solution. It's a marketing approach that looks at traditional advertising media through different eyes. It also makes use of alternative methods of marketing and advertising to help you beef up your results. This new approach was *not* developed in an ivory tower at any major university or mega ad agency. It's a product of the street—not Wall Street, but Main Street. It's called Street Fighter Marketing.

Street Fighter Marketing, or Street Fighting, for short, is *any* efficient, measurable, and low-cost delivery method of an effective message that influences a buying decision culminating in a sale. In some respects, Street Fighting turns marketing back a half century or more to a time when marketing was less inefficient, costly, and confusing. To overcome the increasing inefficiencies of modern marketing, the boundaries between all of these related subsets of marketing (advertising, promotions, public relations, sponsorships, direct mail, sales, and so forth) must become blurred.

> Street Fighter Marketing is any efficient delivery method of an effective message that influences a buying decision culminating in a sale.

You've no doubt heard the term "one-to-one marketing," which is a good first step. But the Street Fighter approach is more aggressive and suggests a totally integrated, individualized approach to attracting and keeping customers. Street Fighter Marketing is the next generation of marketing, developed to combat the deluge of marketing pollution that gets between you and your customers. This is a neighborhood-by-neighborhood, grassroots, in-your-face, take-no-prisoners type of approach that can more accurately be called *One-On-One* Marketing.

Street Fighter Marketing Solutions provides you with a detailed examination of numerous advertising and other marketing tactics. First you'll explore the current and future problems; the reasons that traditional advertising media just isn't giving you the bang for your buck it once did. Then you'll learn solutions to the problem; how to modify, mold, and manipulate traditional advertising methods while supplementing or supplanting them with alternative, novel, and lower-cost/higher-reward marketing techniques. In this way, you will become less dependent on the media but still have it available in your arsenal when the numbers makes sense. You will reach this position by applying your newfound tactical skills in an innovative strategic way that helps you develop the ideal combinations and applications of advertising for your business. The end result is to create a marketing program that costs you much less per each generated transaction. In short, to deliver you more results with your marketing money.

THE PROBLEMS WITH THE FUTURE OF MARKETING

What is the best form of advertising? This question is asked more times than any other at our Street Fighter Marketing seminars and workshops. At the risk of sounding evasive (or like an adult diaper), the answer is "Depends." Nearly every form of advertising *can* be effective, and every form of advertising can be a total waste of your money. It depends on a number of different factors that are specific to your situation. Those variables include your type of business, your marketplace, your position in the marketplace, your brand equity, the season, your product lines, and so on. It's like asking a doctor which drug is the best. It depends on what the ailment is, what other drugs you're taking, what other conditions you have, and your overall health.

I would also like to point out that the question itself is flawed. What should be asked is, "Which form of *marketing* is best?" Advertising is just one part of marketing. Marketing also includes many other tools, like public relations, telemarketing, sales, direct mail, sponsorships, the internet, and a host of others. To continue with the doctor analogy, drugs are just one of the tools at a doctor's disposal. She can also recommend surgery, physical therapy, psychotherapy, nutritional counseling, and exercise or other types of behavior modification. The solutions recommended to a given patient depend on the specific needs of that patient.

Unfortunately, media salespeople often like to play doctor but have one treatment regardless of the problem. And they all want to perform a special surgical procedure called a "cashectomy." It's often done without a proper diagnosis and administered without anesthetic—the three-martini lunch notwithstanding. As a result, in spite of administering a costly remedy, you suffer the same ailment.

Most advertising and marketing have become less effective because the consumer has become increasingly immune to them. While the advertising media is charging more to deliver messages, those messages are less likely to get noticed and remembered. A study by Yankelovich Partners, an American marketing-services consultancy, found that 65 percent of people now feel "constantly bombarded" by ad messages, and 59 percent feel that ads have very little relevance to them. Almost 70 percent said they would be interested in products or services that would help them avoid marketing pitches. Think about that: 70 percent of consumers will spend money to avoid being bombarded with the never-ending proliferation of marketing messages.

"It has been calculated that the average American is subjected to some three thousand advertising messages every day," wrote the authors. "If you add in everything from the stickers on cars to slogans on sweatshirts, and the ads in newspapers, on taxis, and in subways, then some people could be exposed to more than that number just getting to the office. No wonder many consumers seem to be developing the knack of tuning out advertising."

"Consumers are getting harder to influence as commercial clutter invades their lives," says a report by Deutsche Bank. It examined the effectiveness of TV advertising on twenty-three new and mature brands of packaged goods and concluded that in some cases it was a waste of time, not to mention a waste of money. Although TV advertising would lead to a short-term incremental increase in volume sales in almost every case, there was a positive cash return on that investment in only 18 percent of cases. Over a longer term, the picture improved, with 45 percent of cases showing a return on investment. The study concluded that 'increased levels of marketing spending were less important than having new items on the shelf and increasing distribution.'"[1]

Let's examine more closely the reasons that marketing and advertising dollars are rapidly becoming less and less effective. We'll look at two different areas. The first will be the traditional mass media. The second will be a variety of nonmedia-oriented marketing approaches that many businesses attempt to use to increase their overall effectiveness.

TRADITIONAL ADVERTISING MEDIA

The Daily Newspaper

In most markets, the daily newspaper is a primary advertising medium for all types and sizes of local businesses. Despite the major mergers, the increased cost of newsprint, and the downsizing of news staffs, the big problems from an advertiser's standpoint are these:

> Problem: Newspaper circulation is down, yet advertising rates go up.

1. Circulation continues to decline annually.
2. Advertising rates increase annually.
3. Competition increases from alternate sources for news, sports, business, entertainment, and promotion delivery.
4. An attitude of superiority has developed with an inferior service.

According to an article published by Jouralism.org, a media-research organization:

> Newspaper circulation is in decline. The root problems go back to the late 1940s, when the percentage of Americans reading newspapers began to drop. But for years the U.S. population was growing so much that circulation kept rising and then, after 1970, remained stable. That changed in 1990, when circulation began to decline in absolute numbers. And the problem now appears to be more than fewer people developing the newspaper habit. People who used to read every day now read less often. Some people who used to read a newspaper have stopped altogether. Today, just more than half of Americans (54 percent) read a newspaper during the week, somewhat more (62 percent) on Sundays, and the number is continuing to drop.[2]

With circulation declining and readership habits such that your ads are less likely to be seen by readers, you're working with a less efficient medium. Combine that with ever-increasing advertising rates, and it's easy to see that local businesses are spending more money to reach dramatically fewer potential customers. Despite this bleak forecast, there are still times that it might make sense to use newspaper advertising. Even then, however, the managements at the newspapers act as if they had the same monopolistic power in the marketplace as they once enjoyed several decades earlier. This attitude forces local businesses to seek alternative forms of advertising even after initially considering using the local newspaper.

The Consumers' Choice Award in Indianapolis, Indiana (www.ccaindy.com), is a client of ours who has used newspaper advertising successfully for many years. Every year, it would publish a full-color tabloid insert in all of the newspapers in its markets, including the *Indianapolis Star,* promoting the winners of its award. The licensing fee for participating in the program included a quarter-page ad in the tabloid. After several years of the Consumers' Choice Award increasing the number of pages of its insert, the *Star* decided that it wanted to sell the advertising directly to the winners and would not permit the Consumers' Choice Award to publish its insert like it had in years past.

What the management team at the *Star* didn't realize was that most of the participants in the program did not usually buy newspaper advertising. But since it was included in the licensing fee, they were happy to take advantage of it. As a result, the Consumers' Choice Award took that newspaper budget of around $50,000 and used it to purchase advertising time on local television. (This budget will likely double in the next few years.) Much to its delight, the TV campaign made a much bigger impact than the inserts ever did. So even if the *Star* offered to allow the insert again, it would have to drop the price dramatically for the Consumers' Choice Award to consider such a move, based on the newfound return on the marketing investment, or ROMI.[3]

Several of the licensees had never used television advertising before. As a result of this experience, some moved big portions of their marketing budgets from purchasing print to purchasing broadcast space.

Broadcast Television

Local television stations have been a powerful advertising medium to many local businesses over the years. But unlike the daily newspapers, there has been and continues to be some competition among the four major networks and several of the local independent stations. And like the daily newspapers, local television audiences have been eroding at the same time that spot rates have increased. Broadcast television has lost audience to cable, satellite TV, video gaming, and the internet. Remote-control units and digital video recorder (DVR) services like TiVo allow television viewers to avoid viewing commercials.

A survey released by the Association of National Advertisers (ANA) and Forrester Research found that:

78 percent of advertisers feel that traditional television advertising has become less effective in the past two years. The survey also found that marketers are exploring emerging technologies to help bolster their television advertising spending.

Key highlights of the ANA/Forrester survey include:

- Almost 70 percent of advertisers think that DVRs and video-on-demand will reduce or destroy the effectiveness of traditional thirty-second commercials.

- When DVRs spread to thirty million homes, close to 60 percent of advertisers say that they will spend less on conventional TV advertising.

- Advertisers are also looking at alternatives to traditional TV advertising and will spend more of their advertising budgets on: branded entertainment within TV programs (61 percent); TV program sponsorships (55 percent), interactive advertising during TV programs (48 percent), online video ads (45 percent), and product placement (44 percent).[4]

Like the newspaper, local television attracts fewer viewers but charges more, and the viewers that it gets are less likely to even see your commercials. Television still has the power to reach a lot of people, but to get any kind of return, you'll have to think like a Street Fighter.

Cable TV

Local cable television was a great way to supplement a local broadcast TV schedule. For more modest budgets, it was an affordable way to take advantage of sight, sound, and motion in your advertising. At a local level, it could allow you to be on a number of different national television programs. It was affordable, which allowed you to buy enough frequency to get your message remembered. But just as cable television is starting to come into its own as an effective advertising medium, it is being challenged:

> Though cable television remains the predominant technology for the delivery of video programming, cable's share has fallen from almost 100 percent a decade ago to about 75 percent of pay TV subscribers. This is due to competition from direct broadcast satellite TV service, which first became commercially available in 1993. Today almost 22 percent subscribe to a satellite service.[5]

Radio

Radio stations have been very good at combining promotional opportunities with their standard programming. Radio is also the most flexible of the mass advertising media. One of the biggest problems with getting results from radio is that there are just too many choices: choosing the right station (usually based on format like country, talk, top 40, etc.), at the right day-part, with the right number of commercials (frequency), for an effective duration of time (schedule), with the right message (creative). Then you have to factor in what other media and marketing approaches you are using along with it (media mix). Plus, there's one element that often gets overlooked, and that's the cost to reach each member of the listening audience.

This element is generally expressed as the Cost Per Thousand (CPM; "M" stands for one thousand here). In comparing stations, you need to know what you're paying to reach each one thousand listeners of your target audience. Just because a station is rated number one doesn't mean that it's number one for *you*. Too often, the biggest mistake local businesses make with radio is buying too little too often to really make it work. Even if you figure all that out, you have to come up with a message that gets the job done for you.

In the face of all those choices, radio may be also suffering from an erosion of its audience. A local radio now competes with satellite radio, audio CDs, DVDs, iPods, cell phones, and global positioning system (GPS).

> Bridge Ratings recently did a study to see what effect MP3 players are having on radio listenership among twelve- to eighteen-year olds. Not surprisingly, people who owned players have tuned in less since the purchase of their MP3 player. They also mention in an earlier study that listeners are listening to a wider variety of music genres, forcing radio stations to change their programming.[6]

Yet radio is perhaps the most affordable of all the major mass media, and it's one of the most flexible as well. But just because you can afford to buy it doesn't mean you are going to see a return on your investment. We've had attendees at our seminars tell us that they tried radio, and it didn't work for them. Their assumption was that radio doesn't work. In fact, they didn't use the medium correctly to get results.

Outdoor Advertising

Due to the increasing restrictions for new billboards by most communities, there is a shrinking amount of good inventory

in outdoor advertising. Limited supply means that you'll probably pay a premium for it. Even with some of the other outdoor
alternatives, like wrapped buses, mall posters, phone kiosks, taxi
tops, and truck side panels, your message has to be painfully
simple to work. For that reason, outdoor advertising is generally
better suited to national advertisers with a high degree of existing brand awareness. For local advertisers on a limited budget,
it's often too costly and too limiting to get a return. The cost of
the production alone (usually a full-color vinyl covering) can
cost as much as a month of exposure.

Yellow Pages Directories

It's not uncommon for a small business to devote half its advertising budget to yellow pages advertising. This used to be a must-buy
for any type of local, community, or neighborhood service company. When there was a problem—your furnace was broken, your
toilet was backed up, or you had to get your grease trap cleaned at
your restaurant—you usually let your fingers do the walking. But
this approach has changed with the proliferation of directories
and web-based or cell-phone-based alternatives.

Yellow pages advertising was always expensive, but often a
necessary evil. Plus, its sales force often approached your business like storm troopers, using scare tactics to get you to buy
and buy big. And once you made a decision, you were stuck with
it for an entire year.

**Weeklies, Tabloids, and Other Miscellaneous
Print Advertising**

Many options exist: local magazines and suburban newspapers; specialty publications and *Pennysaver*; and bowling sheets,
church or school bulletins, and event programs. These options

are not really what I would consider major mass media, but they are often part of the media mix. In reality, this type of advertising is the proverbial black hole of marketing. It sucks up a lot of marketing dollars, and what is returned is often a mystery.

NONTRADITIONAL MARKETING

Now that we've looked at the traditional advertising media, the next area that needs to be explored covers the nontraditional forms of marketing that can eat up huge chunks of your budget.

Direct mail

In 2004 American businesses spent $52.5 billion advertising their products and services using direct mail. Households received 144.5 billion pieces of mail. Direct mail advertising spending increased 8 percent in 2004, outpacing the growth in newspaper, radio, and total advertising spending.[7] That's a lot of money to spend on "junk mail." Yet, with the ever-increasing sheer volume of direct mail advertising, it becomes increasingly challenging to get your potential customers to respond to your mail piece.

> Media is not enough. You need to supplement it or replace some of it with more efficient alternative forms of marketing.

There are three different reasons why your direct mail advertising is more likely to bypass the reader on its way to the recycling bin (not necessarily in this order):

1. A weak, untargeted, out-of-date mailing list;
2. A poorly written and produced mailing piece;
3. Lack of proper research and testing.

A local business is more likely to shoot from the hip with a direct mail campaign, using what we often refer to as the "spray and pray" approach. Street Fighters, on the other hand, know that direct mail can be powerful if the effort is taken to ensure that it is done properly. The reason direct mail is not used more is because there is no one knocking on your door to sell you the service. With newspaper, radio, yellow pages, TV, and other mass advertising, there are sales forces that proactively go after your business. They make it easy for you to buy. That is not the case with alternative forms of marketing. You have to initiate various programs like direct mail. Can you imagine a sales call from the postal service?

Internet

The internet is new, exciting, necessary, and can end up causing you to waste tens of thousands of dollars. This new-age marketing tool is so new that the rules, the tools, and the metrics are being rewritten on a weekly basis. A Street Fighter Marketing Solution will likely include some use of the internet. The key is balancing your greatest possible return against your investment in both time and money.

There are many different ways of sinking your marketing dollars down this electronic well. A really good, functional website can end up costing a small fortune to develop. Once you get it started, it often takes on a life of its own. It requires more and more updating and maintenance. Every little change and improvement costs more money.

Other marketing avenues include spam, pop-ups, banner ads, blogs, e-commerce, and e-zines. Just as new avenues for sending advertising messages via the internet open up, companies develop software to block those messages. There are sponsored links on Google, MSN, Yahoo, and other search engines or browsers where you pay per click (PPC). There are unique URLs and other sites to help you promote and sell, including eBay, Amazon, and Overstock. As a Street Fighter, you will learn which of these online approaches make the most sense for you.

Telephone Marketing and Telemarketing

This once powerful tool has been significantly dulled by new laws. Do-not-call lists, caller ID, "call blockers," and cell phones that create less reliance on landlines have sent this marketing powerhouse into the outhouse. Yet there are still opportunities. Regardless of the difficulties, some form of telephone marketing is usually an efficient way of beefing up your marketing.

Local companies usually don't think about the inbound element of telephone marketing. You can spend money on all of these marketing programs to motivate a customer to call you, but if that inbound inquiry is fielded unprofessionally, you can lose those potential customers even with the advertising doing what it's supposed to do. Answering machines, voice mail, automated call attendants, and interactive voice response (IVR) systems are just as frustrating as talking to an inept, undertrained, disinterested receptionist.

A Street Fighter knows that you have one shot at a potential customer when that person calls your business. This point of first contact is critical, yet it is often the weakest link in the marketing chain for most businesses, large and small.

Selling

Selling and marketing don't get along. The sales force and the marketing staff are usually at odds in many organizations. A Street Fighter, however, views the sales staff as one more marketing tool. A Street Fighter also recognizes that in smaller companies there may not be a person with the title of "salesperson." But there are people in nearly every business who must do some kind of selling as part of their responsibilities. The selling function is oftentimes the final step in the marketing process of getting that customer to buy for the first time. Asking for the order can be as elaborate as getting the final paperwork that closes the deal on a dozen jumbo jets, or it could be as simple as "Would you like fries with that?" It's all selling.

Consider this example: Many years ago, while working for a small advertising agency, I convinced my father into letting me do a small direct mail campaign to promote the family business: an office coffee service. I created a direct mail campaign with a series of mailers. The photography, layout, design, and printing were done on trade for coffee, so that there was little out-of-pocket cost except for the mailing list and postage. I then used some eye-catching headlines, including: "My Coffee Is Worth Beans" and "Use My Bunns Free." (Bunn was the brand name of the coffeemaker my father used.)

The mailers generated several inbound inquiries. One was from a major mortgage company that used sixteen boxes of coffee a month. My father's largest customers at that time used only five boxes of coffee a month. This campaign had created a lead of significant size. My father made the phone calls, answered some questions, and gave some prices, but he never followed up. He wasn't a salesman. They never called back, so the opportunity just faded away. Did the advertising work? It did in the sense that it generated a good lead. However, an overall marketing campaign, which must include a sales effort and a follow-up, wasn't implemented at all. Consequently, the total program failed. The bottom line is that the integrated marketing program did not end up providing a return on the marketing investment, even though the investment was very small in real dollars.

Now consider an example from an industry that focuses on

its salespeople: Jeannie, our office manager, went shopping for a midsize four-door sedan. She told each salesman that with only two kids, it was important to her to have a car that seated six people, but she did *not* want a minivan. Five of the six salesmen kept trying to sell her a minivan. "They wouldn't listen to me," she said. "I told them I did not want a minivan, but as soon as they found out I was a mother of two, they kept pitching me the minivan." The dealership that ultimately got the sale was the one where the salesmen listened to what she wanted and never mentioned anything about a minivan.

Advertising Agencies

Ad agencies deal with both the media and the creation of the message. They usually like to think of themselves as full-service marketing companies. The message of your marketing is just as important as the delivery of that message. You'll spend a certain amount of money getting that message out to your potential buyers. That investment can generate many new customers or none, depending on how effective the message was.

The problem with small local advertising agencies is that most of them dream of being large national advertising agencies. It's a creative business, but sometimes the creativity gets in the way of the selling message.

Consider how advertising messages are recognized by the advertising industry. It's not based on the return on investment to the client. The advertising is evaluated by several different advertising organizations. The two most prominent award programs are the Clios and the ADDYs.

The Clios seem to focus more on a national and international level, whereas the ADDYs also have a strong presence in local communities. When you get a pitch from an advertising agency, one of the first things it touts are the awards it has won.

But what does winning these awards mean to your bottom line? Go to the Clio Awards website. It says:

> The essence of Clio: to recognize the people and programs at the ever-changing vanguard. As the industry progresses, the Clio Awards has evolved, recognizing the new dynamics of the ad marketplace and rewarding the work that is leading the industry forward.

Now go to the website for the the American Advertising Federation ADDY Awards. The ADDYs are the advertising industry's largest and most representative competition, attracting over fifty thousand entries every year in local ADDY competitions. Its website says:

> The mission of the ADDY competition is to recognize and reward creative excellence in the art of advertising.

Notice that nowhere in these descriptions of their awards does it mention any kind of return on investment.

Also, consider that the most award-winning and memorable campaign of the 1990s was "Got milk?" Yet milk consumption went down every year from 1990 to 1999.

To be fair, there are many good advertising agencies. Some are good for specific types of clients. Accountability for the results of the advertising should be first and foremost in their minds.

The Message Must Reflect Reality

One other problem is that an agency can come up with a wonderful slogan, but that doesn't mean that what happens at the point of sale reflects the message sent. I've been to a Radio Shack and got *no answers* to my questions. I've been to a McDonald's where they couldn't have cared less if I smiled. Sprint keeps touting "free and clear." I'm a Sprint PCS customer, and I know firsthand it's certainly not free, and many times the signal is not clear. And one of the most annoying missteps comes from the car companies that market to women but then have salesmen at the dealerships treat women poorly.

From the agency, to its corporate client, to the point of the final sale, the message has to be consistent and accurate. Just because something is presented in advertising doesn't make it true in the real world, which is why there is a distrust of advertising.

As a subset to advertising agencies, there are all those vendors that market their unique services. These include production houses, animators, jingle writers and producers, photographers, graphic artists, copywriters, and so on. Each pushes his own service. The account executive working for a jingle company is selling jingles. Do you need a jingle? Could the jingle money be used more effectively elsewhere?

The same goes for your logo. Most logos used by local businesses don't make any sense. I've seen hundreds of random designs that have no meaning. The business owners are proud of their logos. Nonetheless, like any other form of marketing, a logo has to do a job. It has to help sell.

Co-op Advertising

Free money is being wasted. It's yours for the taking. Companies that offer co-op advertising plans for their products cover the retail spectrum, from cars to computers to cosmetics. There is $50 billion available in co-op funds, plus over one thousand manufacturer programs that reimburse 100 percent of your qualified advertising expenditures, according to the *Co-op Advertising Programs Sourcebook*. But according to the Yellow Pages Publishers Association (YPPA), a significant amount of this money goes unused. Many retailers fail to use available funds because they are unaware of them or believe that qualifying for them would be too difficult.[8]

Publicity

The most common misconception is that publicity is free. It's not. It is true that there is no cost paid to media for the placement of a message, but there are other costs to create news releases and collateral material, and time is needed to pitch the story to the press.

Having said that, publicity can provide great value compared to traditional advertising. The downside is that you have no control over the message. In spite of its advantages, publicity is an overlooked opportunity for many local businesses. Time is the issue. You don't have the time or know-how to suggest a newsworthy story to the press, and the opportunity is lost. You can hire a PR firm to do it for you, and more times than not, you won't get your ROI (return on investment). The news media is besieged by countless requests, and on a local level, you have a finite number of decent press outlets for your stories.

The biggest advantage of getting a story is that it is more credible than advertising. The news is the very reason people read publications, and watch or listen to the news. If you can become part of the news, you potentially make a big impact. But reporters are not interested in providing your business with free advertising. Street Fighters know how to present their story idea so that a reporter will be interested. Street Fighters also work publicity into their overall marketing programs. And this integration provides leverage that yields an impressive multiple on your invested marketing dollars.

Conventions, Tradeshows, and Exhibitions

These events are a major expense for many companies because they involve all the different types of corporate communications. The most involved is the annual convention. Generally, once a year, a company will bring in its frontline people. That could be its franchisees, store managers, dealers, and agents, along with vendors and the corporate support people. It is an opportunity to introduce new ideas, procedures, products, and services. It also is used to fire up the troops and help different groups network. With the massive cost of one of these events, it is critical that companies and organizations demand a much higher return on their investment. The major wastes are:

Big-name Celebrity Keynote Speakers

A former sports star or coach, national newsperson, political personality, or movie star costs a lot of money. Having one present will create buzz at your event. Is that the best use of your marketing dollars? Granted, Terry Bradshaw is an entertaining speaker. Lou Holtz is a powerful speaker. But other than some generic sports-related teamwork, overcoming-obstacles, goal-setting stuff, their message has no direct value to a business audience. Do General Norman Schwarzkopf's stories about motivating his troops really have a direct bearing on motivating *your* troops? Or, more to the point, could that six-figure cost be put to a more effective use?

Boring Industry Speakers

They may be able to present the right information, but if the audience is asleep, are you really getting your ROMI (return on marketing investment) for having your attendees in that breakout session?

Big-name Entertainment

A convention is an opportunity to inform, teach, train, excite, and motivate employees, dealers, vendors, and franchisees.

Exposing them to information does not get them to remember or act upon that information. If you bring in Huey Lewis and the News for your Saturday night entertainment, it will get talked about. But what will your attendees leave with? How will they better sell, market, promote, and bring in new customers after singing along with "I Want a New Drug"?

A Street Fighter will plan each event from beginning to end so that her business will get maximum results for the least amount of money. You can still offer maximum entertainment value and at the same time reinforce your critical messages.

Consumer Shows

Local businesses spend a lot of money participating in these specialty shows. They may include car shows, home shows, lawn and garden shows, boat shows, and so on. In theory, they're a great way to get many would-be buyers to come see your booth and learn about your products and services. But what is the return? First, you have to look at all the expenses connected to participating in the show. The booth fee is only a small part of it. If you want electricity, you have to pay a union person to plug in your cord. Then, there's the added cost of transporting all your stuff to the site, the cost to staff the booth, and the costs of having a compelling, eye-catching display and giveaways at your booth.

Now, in spite of all the time and expenses of participating in a show, most participants have no strategy for turning the thousands of lookers into buyers. Of course, some will have a free drawing so they can generate a database with the information they collect, but, all too often, they don't convert that effort into sales. According to the Center for Exhibition Industry Research, 88 percent of exhibition attendees did not receive follow-up phone calls in 2000. Trade shows can be effective only if the opportunities are followed up.

Sponsorships

A lot of money is spent on local sponsorships. It could be for sporting events or fund-raisers. There's usually some media exposure, and logos are displayed—plus my favorite, the T-shirt with twenty-seven tiny logos all over it. Most sponsorship money is a total waste. Often, because it supports a local worthy cause, the ROI is not held to the same standards as traditional advertising. Perhaps this is because the money comes out of a different budget. As a Street Fighter, you need to examine each potential sponsorship opportunity and structure the arrangement so that you can maximize the return. If you're not getting buying customers from your involvement with a sponsorship, your money should be put elsewhere.

Advertising Specialties and Promotional Products

According to the Professional Products Association International, promotional products make up a $17.3 billion industry. That's a lot of tchotchkes. These items can be anything that can carry a logo or slogan, from caps to cups, keepsakes, coasters, clocks, combs, clips, chairs, and a million other types of crap. Yes, they can help customers remember your business name or give you something to talk about at your trade show or sales call. But unless you incorporate your give-aways and getaways into your overall Street Fighter Marketing strategy, they're just trinkets, toys, and trash. For most small businesses, it may cost only a few hundred here and there, but it adds up and, if not used effectively, squanders valuable resources that could be more readily used to bring customers in the front door.

FINI

These are some major problems with marketing, and they're going to get worse. In the near future, the traditional advertising media will become less cost effective for most average businesses. The nontraditional marketing approaches will become increasingly difficult to adapt and manage. You'll be besieged by throngs of salespeople touting stats that prove their station, publication, or cyber offers will bring you business. To make your marketing and advertising money work smarter, you'll need to reevaluate *all* of your marketing. Though it's impossible to start with a clean slate, you can start with a fresh focus called "zero-based marketing." Look for alternatives and supplements in places you never thought of before. You'll need to examine different and unique approaches to marketing that all work synergistically while seamlessly functioning within your operation. Now that you see most of the problems, you can start working on your Street Fighter strategies, plans, tactics, and *solutions*. That's what this book is about.

2

SHOW ME THE ROMI
(Return on Marketing
Investment)

What is a successful marketing program? Most business people would probably tell you it's one that generates new customers or increased sales. But how do you know if your marketing program is doing its job? Figuring that out is tougher. According to Gerald Garcia Jr., president and CEO of AIMS Worldwide, a vertically integrated marketing solutions services company:

The key measurements of your marketing program must include tangible benefits such as revenue or profit or customer activity. It's not enough to justify it with cost efficiencies in media buying or subjective "measurement" of creative programs.

> If your accountant
> wouldn't endorse it,
> you should divorce it.
> If your accountant
> wouldn't advise it,
> you should excise it.

The first step in developing your Street Fighter Marketing program is to determine what your desired end result is in any or all given marketing components, as well as for your overall marketing program. To do that, all of your marketing initiatives must have some tracking capabilities. You will also need to be able to calculate how much you're willing to invest to generate a new customer or expand your sales from an existing customer. Doing so helps you calculate your return on marketing dollars invested.

ACCOUNTABILITY

Your marketing results must be measurable to be practical. Without measurability, there's no accountability. Without accountability, you can't calculate your ROMI. And without calculating your ROMI, you can't determine if you're getting your money's worth. Therefore you need the means to determine if all of your various forms of marketing are getting the desired results. If you can't incorporate a tracking procedure that allows you to measure the results of your marketing, you're at risk of wasting money, time, and opportunity.

Before you commit to do another marketing program, ask what your accountant would say. My baby brother, Howard Slutsky, is a certified public accountant. He's a numbers guy—conservative, boring. He is a bean counter and proud of it. He's not creative or intuitive. If I can't prove it to him on paper that a given marketing approach makes sense, he shakes his head with disapproval. So before we spend money on marketing, I ask "What would Howard say?" Now the same pragmatic approach to marketing is working its way up the corporate ladder.

> Ask yourself "What would Howard say?"

> Those heady days of blind budget increases are fast being replaced with a new mantra: measurement and accountability.

Armed with reams of data, increasingly sophisticated tools, and growing evidence that the old tricks simply don't work, there's hardly a marketing executive today who isn't demanding a more scientific approach to help defend marketing strategies in front of the chief financial officer. Marketers want to know the actual return on investment of each dollar. They want to know it often, not just annually. And, increasingly, they want a view of likely returns on future campaigns. The push is coming from the top ranks. CEOs, CFOs, and even board directors have relentlessly cut costs in every corner of their *companies except marketing and are fed up with funneling cash into TV commercials and glossy ads that they say cost more and seem to do less.* That's especially true at a time when profits are under attack and consumers of all ages are zapping ads and spending more time playing video games and surfing the internet. The bean counters know that marketing matters. But they're hazy about how much or what kind.[9]

MACRO ROMI

No, it's not an imitation Italian dish made with pasta and cheese. It's a bird's-eye view of your marketing's effectiveness and a good place to start learning how to generate a good return on your marketing investment.

Add up all the expenditures directly related to your marketing. Include all traditional advertising, plus community involvement programs such as church bulletins, high school newspapers, Little League sponsorships, and Main Street festivals. If you've purchased any specialty items with your logo on them, like pens, T-shirts, coffee cups, key chains, refrigerator magnets, and so on, put them in the pot. If you have provided in-kind support, include your cost of donating the product or service. Don't forget your yellow pages ads, message on hold, internal telemarketers, salespeople, giveaways (like tickets to concerts), or lunches with prospects. Oh! And don't forget your basic marketing billboard promotional piece: your business cards.

Add any design work, such as logo development and website design. Also assign an appropriate amount for items you use for multiple purposes, including marketing (for example, stationery) and add that amount to your marketing costs. Once you add up the prices of all the items, you will have an accurate idea of your marketing costs. Compare it against your total gross and net sales.

Now, what would happen if you could get the same level of sales and cut your marketing budget in half? Street Fighter Marketing Solutions will do just that for you. But you will have to make some tough choices and difficult changes.

Calculating Your ROMI

In his book *Return on Marketing Investment*,[10] Guy R. Powell defines ROMI as "revenue (or margin) generated by a marketing program divided by the cost of the program at a given risk level." This definition works fine for big companies with major budgets. However, since the focus of my book is marketing at the Street Fighter level, the ROMI definition we use is simply "revenue generated by a marketing program divided by the cost of that program." The Street Fighter definition allows you to express your ROMI as a specific dollar amount or as a percentage.

Powell also factors in another element that he calls the "hurdle rate," which he defines as the minimum acceptable, expected return of a marketing program at a given level of risk. You don't need to take into account the hurdle rate when following the Street Fighter Marketing Solution. For most marketing programs executed on the local level, you simply need to know how much revenue you generated in relation to what it cost you to generate it.

The Street Fighter way uses the same method you would use to evaluate a return on any investment, be it marketing or a new delivery van or a third store. The investment costs you X. That investment generates Y, which is sales, profit, new customers, or whatever other criteria you use to measure company performance. You subtract X from Y, and the product is your ROMI. You can express it in real dollars or as a percentage, depending on your objectives.

Consider this example: A radio schedule costs you $5,000. You are promoting a specific product at a specific price that is not being advertised or marketed anywhere else. Consequently, customers who request that deal are most likely to be responding to the radio advertising. There is $10,000 worth of sales for that product. Assume that half the customers who came to buy that product also bought additional items worth another $3,000 in sales. Your immediate return on gross sales is $13,000 less $5,000 or $8,000 (simple enough to figure out for the radio investment).

But you should also factor in the direct cost of the goods sold. If your average margin was 50 percent, the gross profit generated from this particular radio schedule would be $6,500. The return, therefore, would be $6,500 less $5,000, or $1,500. You could say either that the advertising was profitable or that there was a 30 percent return.

There are other considerations when calculating ROMI. For example, of those customers who bought as a result of that radio schedule, how many of them are first-time buyers with your business? If a total of 100 customers spent $13,000, and 25 of them are new customers, you have to look at a few other numbers to determine the ROMI:

1. Of the 75 regular customers, how many of them would have purchased that item had you promoted it with less expensive

marketing, such as like counter displays, targeted postcard mailers to customers, or statement stuffers?
2. Did you offer a discount or value added? If so, determine how many of the regular customers, would have paid full price if there hadn't been a promotion.
3. Track how many of the 25 new customers return again and become your regular customers. If you were able to determine that 15 of the 25 new customers become regulars, your ROMI for that particular radio schedule would be much higher. To figure exactly how much higher, though, you would have to know what a new customer is worth to your business.

What's a New Customer Worth to You?

It's strange, but many small-business people have no idea what a good regular customer is worth to their business. By calculating that, you should gain a better idea of what you're willing to invest or risk to attract a good regular customer. It also tells you how important it is to keep your existing customers happy. The cost of retaining a customer and even expanding a customer's value is much less costly than finding a new customer.

To determine what you're willing to invest in marketing, first discover what an average new customer is worth to you. To determine the value, answer the following questions:

1. What is your average sale (transaction amount)?
2. What is the frequency of your average customer? This calculation can be expressed in transactions or visits per week, month, or year, depending on the type of operation you run.
3. What percentage of new customers become average regular customers? This will undoubtedly vary, depending on how

that new customer was generated. For example, someone buying for the first time using an aggressively priced coupon is less likely be a repeat customer than one who bought based on a friend's personal recommendation. To be more accurate, you may want to calculate this information based on several different criteria. Then once you have the numbers for three or four scenarios, take an average.

4. What is the average life cycle of a new customer? That is, once you get a customer, how long will that customer continue to buy from you before he or she moves, gets mad, or no longer has a need for your product or service? This length of time can generally be expressed in months or years. It may be a more difficult number to calculate, but do your best.

5. How many new customers are referred to you by your existing customers? When you gather information about a new customer, ask how he found out about you. One possible answer is "referred by a friend."

When calculating your return, consider that there are three main types of ROMI:

1. Immediate ROMI
2. Long-term ROMI
3. Multi-input ROMI

Immediate ROMI is the return you get on a given marketing event. That would be the dollars generated directly from the sales related to that promotion. In the earlier example, the immediate ROMI was $1,500, or 30 percent. It's always good when your marketing shows an immediate profit. It doesn't always work that way. You could have spent $5,000 and generated $3,000 of total sales. That's $1,500 of actual margin and a loss of $3,500.

Long-term ROMI takes into account all of the sales generated from a new customer over that customer's life cycle. In the example above, you generated 15 new customers. For those 15 new customers, look at the following numbers:

1. Your average sale is $100.
2. Your average customer frequency is once a week.
3. Your average customer life cycle is two years.
4. You get one new referral for every two new customers.

Assuming these are accurate numbers, those 15 new customers represent about $1,500 in new sales per week. They buy an average of fifty times during the year, or provide you with $75,000 in sales. They stay with you for two years, so double the amount of sales to $150,000. You work on a 50 percent margin, so your gross profit is $75,000. You can also make a case for an additional $37,500 that will be generated from the referrals you get from those 15 new customers.

Even if the immediate ROMI is a loss, you may be able to see that in the long term your marketing will eventually show you a return. But you can't sustain those kinds of losses for too long.

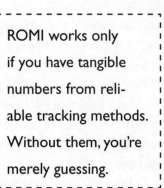

ROMI works only if you have tangible numbers from reliable tracking methods. Without them, you're merely guessing.

Your ROMI numbers are only as good as the raw data you consider. Don't guess. You must have a tangible way of proving the numbers you use. Without tracking and data capture, it's all just guesswork, and that's worthless. Wrong numbers are worse then no numbers at all because they will mislead you. We call this "phony ROMI."

Armed with this type of information and a strong tracking

system, you can begin to figure out what your ROMI will be on any single promotion or promotional campaign. As mentioned before, just about any form of marketing or advertising can be effective or ineffective, depending on a number of elements. One of those elements is the cost of the promotion. If you ran a local radio campaign that cost you $2,500, and it generated 15 new customers, your immediate return would be $1,500, or a $1000 loss. But if you determine that half your new customers became regulars, you could justify that advertising expense, because over time, it will have paid for itself.

On the other hand, if the campaign focused on a price and item that brought in only the bargain hunters, it's likely that the radio ads lost money.

There are several different ways of gathering the information you need to calculate your ROMI.

Multi-input ROMI

If your ad appears in a monthly magazine each month for a year, do your sales from each ad increase each month? If so, you may have to factor in the benefit of the repetition of that ad. Perhaps the first few insertions lost money, but by the third month, it had started generating net profits. The third ad shows a positive ROMI. In such a case, you may want to calculate your ROMI based on the entire schedule of ads in that publication. It's likely that the results you're getting in months three through twelve would not have been as strong without the first two ads that lost money.

Making these calculations is more complicated when you mix the media. It is possible for a customer to see your front sign, read a newspaper ad, observe several of your delivery trucks with your logo, talk to a friend who recommends you, and then look you up in the yellow pages. When that customer is asked

"How did you find out about us?" he might respond with the last marketing contact: "yellow pages." But that sale would not have happened if it weren't for most, if not all, of all those previous impressions.

The point is that capturing this information is not perfect. Just be aware of the limitations as you begin to put the information to use.

TRACKING DEVICES

Redemption

Redeeming a printed piece that has value when used in a purchase is an easy and accurate way of evaluating printed forms of marketing, including print media, direct mail, group coupon mailers, and so on.

Consider Steve, the manager of a Back Yard Burgers franchise in Tennessee. He arranged for a Blockbuster Video down the street to hand out a certificate to each of its customers for one week. To get the special offer, a customer had to come in with the cross-promotion certificate. The number of certificates redeemed tells you only half the story. There were about two hundred redemptions. But not all that came in were new customers.

Steve simply had his counter people ask everyone who redeemed the Blockbuster certificate if it was their first visit. If it was, the counter person marked it on the certificate and attached that certificate to the sale receipt. In that way, Steve could determine exactly, to the penny, the level of new immediate sales that were generated from that promotion. His bounce-back coupon also allowed him to determine who came in for a second time.

To analyze the true value of a promotion, distill the number of new customers from the redemptions. If you have a regular customer already, you don't want to discount that regular customer if he or she would be willing to pay full price to begin with. This point is particularly more important for marketing on a local level. Another consideration is whether a regular customer's use of the certificate increased the frequency of his visits.

You've probably figured that Steve's ROMI was very high, since the cost of the entire promotion was about $25. These types of lower-cost alternatives to more expensive media advertising will be explored in later chapters.

When you get down to it, there are really only four ways to increase your sales on a local level:

1. Increase your customer count. (Get more customers.)
2. Increase your customer frequency. (Get them to buy more often.)
3. Increase your average transaction value. (Get them to spend more money each time.)
4. Convert current purchases into more products or services with higher profit margins.

If your marketing tactic positively impacts one or all four of these areas, you can show a strong return, which we refer to as "worthy ROMI."

Any degree of worthy ROMI will usually involve tracking your marketing tactic in one of four ways:

1. The number of visits to your location
2. The number of inbound phone calls
3. The number of mail-in, fax, or email requests or orders
4. The number of unique (unduplicated) visitors that log on to your website

All four of these require a "call to action" in the marketing proposition. In turn, each action allows you to gather the information you need to begin to determine the quantitative value of your marketing. With e-commerce, for example, you can easily track where all your sales came from, as well as the activity the customer does on your site. It also allows for data capture, which is very important for follow-up marketing of all types, to be addressed in greater detail later.

Direct mail and direct response advertising, where the product is purchased directly as a result of the advertisement, is also easily tracked. The challenge comes from most other forms of marketing, which are not as easily tracked. Below are some common approaches that can help you begin to get an idea of what level of sales is generated from which marketing approaches.

Coupon Promotion

A coupon is the one of the easiest ways of tracking. It has to accompany the purchase. It generally saves money or increases value, giving the customer a reason to bring it in. Determining if the coupon user is a new customer or not requires more effort, though. You must train your frontline staff to ask, "Is this your first time in our store?" The answer then needs to be recorded on the coupon or on a tally sheet. Whether a customer is new or existing is an important piece of information for getting a real accurate ROMI. Discounting your regular customers, who probably would have paid full price anyway, is not the best way to increase your sales. It's OK to do that when necessary, however. If a given coupon promotion has one hundred redemptions and generates ten new customers, it's probably going to have a positive ROMI.

Advertising Codes and Extension Numbers

For print advertising, including newspaper, magazine, and direct mail, you can use a promotional code or a unique phone number or email address to determine which ad was responsible for customer contact. In your call to action, include the special code. If the reader is taking advantage of a special offer in your ad, he must give you the promotional code to receive the offer. The code tells you which ad generated the sale.

For a coupon or ad that is either mailed in or brought to your location, the code is still important. You can run the same ad in several publications over a period of time. By making the promotional code unique to each insertion, you can track which publication or edition brought in the business.

Once you know the medium responsible for the contact, you can track the purchases of that contact to figure out the ROMI for that ad. Getting several hundred phone calls is not enough. How many of those phone calls resulted in sales? Only when you know that can you figure out if the ads are really working for you.

Specific to Product

When introducing a new product or service, gross sales of that product or service can easily be compared to the cost of generating those sales. Steve at Back Yard Burgers started a kids' night on Wednesdays. Kids eat free when accompanied by a paying adult. He brought in a clown, toy giveaways, and a Moonwalk inflatable each Wednesday, spending an additional $150 for the extras. (He was able to get a trial rate for the Moonwalk: four weeks at $50 per week, including setup.) The marketing was done internally to existing customers and on an outside marquee sign. Assuming he's running a 50 percent profit on food, paper, and labor costs, he needs to generate at least $300 more on Wednesdays to break even. With an increase of, let's say, $600, there would be a ROMI of 25 percent on gross sales ($150 cost into $600 in additional sales). That's pretty strong. So in this case, the increase in sales came mainly from existing customers buying more often.

With this type of tracking method, it's possible that you'll get more response than you will actually record. A customer might have intended to bring his children one night but couldn't for some reason. Yet because he had top-of-mind awareness as a result of the promotion, he may come in the next day for lunch. (*Top-of-mind awareness* is when the consumers in your marketplace consider your particular product or services one of the few choices when purchasing.) In that case, the kids' program would have generated an additional sale at lunchtime, but it would not likely be included in any tracking program except the macro-ROMI calculations.

Specific Call to Action

In your advertising, ask the consumers to take a specific course of action. It could be to call a certain number or visit a website. You could get a rough idea by comparing the overall volume of calls or hits prior to the marketing program with those after the marketing program. Or you could provide consumers with a specific number to call or URL to visit, which would give you a more accurate take on the activity generated from the marketing.

Unique Toll-free Numbers

Toll-free numbers are very inexpensive. They are simply forwarded into your regular phone lines. Most providers charge you only for the actual calling time of the inbound call. The advantage is that if you assign a certain toll-free number to a specific marketing campaign, any calls on that number are automatically tracked for you. You monthly bill will even give a list of phone numbers that were used in calling your toll-free number. This setup is good not only for tracking but for creating a very inexpensive follow-up marketing program, including enhancing your database marketing program. There will be more on this later.

Consumer Research

Consumer research can determine if there is an increase in overall awareness of a product, service, or business. The problem is that is very costly and generally can't be applied to specific advertising. So for most small businesses, it is impractical. However, for the savvy Street Fighter, sometimes you can get a local college that offers a marketing research course to take you on as a class project. Just make sure that the questionnaire it uses will not bias the answers you get.

MANAGING THE TRACKING INITIATIVE

In your business, you need to have your frontline people ask questions of your customers and document the results. It has to be clear that this is not a volunteer assignment. Make it easy for them with a simple tracking sheet that requires very few entries. I prefer to use one that uses simple tick marks so that it takes minimal time for the counter people or inbound phone staff to capture that information.

You also will need to spot-check their efforts. Just because you tell them they must record this information doesn't mean that it will get done. I suggest a carrot-and-stick method. Send a "mystery shopper" into your place. If the counter person does the marketing data capture properly, the mystery shopper hands over a $20 bill on the spot. The word will get out real quick. Conversely, if the counter person does not capture the data properly, the shopper hands over a memo in the shape of a $20 bill that tells the person he or she just lost out on a nice spiff. Likewise, the word will get out real quick.

For the phone staff, it should work similarly. The manager could have an envelope with a $20 bill in it. Only the mystery phone shopper and the manager would know the secret password. When the phone staff captures the right information, the caller identifies himself/herself and tells the phone staff the password so he/she can tell the supervisor. The envelope is handed over on the spot. But if the phone staff does not handle the call properly, the phone staff is given a different password. The supervisor hands over a different envelope with a note explaining that it could have been a $20 bill.

THE UNTRACKABLE

What if you have a marketing program that has no effective way of being tracked? According to B. Joseph Vincent, vice chairman of the board for AIMS Worldwide, "At AIMS we have a doctrine that states, 'If we cannot measure it, we will not recommend it. Period.'"

First you need to assess the level of risk involved. For a local business, if such a program costs $10,000, that would be high risk. If it costs $50, it's low risk. Obviously, you have to adjust the number for your marketplace and business. For the higher-risk marketing ventures that are not traceable, the answer is simple: stop it. If you can't track it,

> If you can't track it,
> you must sack it.
> If you can't rate it,
> you must hate it.
> If you can't quantify it,
> you must disqualify it.

don't do it. On the other hand, if it costs you very little money and time, and you have a good feeling about it—also stop it.

With limited budgets, you can't afford to guess what works and what doesn't. Only choose those marketing approaches that have the ability to prove their value to you. If it's not provable, it's not valuable.

There may be marketing that is not provable that works great. The problem is that you'll never know it. As a local business, you have to be picky about where you put your limited resources for marketing.

Once you've figured out all these numbers related to your marketing, you will have a valuable piece of information at your disposal. It's like knowing the actual dealer's cost of a car before negotiating the final price. The calculations tell you several things. First, they let you know if you're improving the efficiency of your marketing. Second, they give you a guide when evaluating the cost of a new marketing program. If that radio-station salesperson comes to you with a $5,000 proposal, you may now know that it makes sense to you only if that investment can generate, let's say, $15,000 worth of sales. You know from past experience that it has generated about $10,000 in sales. Given that, you should be willing to pay only $3,330 for that schedule to make it work for you. If the rep doesn't play ball, you simply find an alternative marketing approach that fits within your guidelines. Either way, you are working to improve your ROMI. Improved ROMI results in improved Earnings Before Interest, Taxes, Depreciation, and Amortization (EBITDA).

3

MAXIMIZING YOUR LOCAL MASS MEDIA

It's likely that a significant portion of your marketing budget is devoted to some type of mass advertising media. As mentioned before, the mass advertising media has been eroding. Newspapers and local affiliate television stations have been losing audience. Many radio stations have experienced the same thing. Your once single local yellow pages directory has spun off more clones than the TV hit *Law & Order*. Even so, the audience sizes are still significant enough to make a major impact in your marketplace. The problem is the cost.

If the cost to reach each one thousand members of a target audience allows you to show a good return on your investment, then the mass media is a great way to go. But what's been happening is that rates continue to rise in the face of declining audience numbers. In short, it costs more to buy less. It's like increasing the cost of a Snickers bar while, at the same time, the manufacturer decreases the candy bar's weight. It then takes a Snickers plus half a Mounds bar to provide the same amount of sugar rush.

Another problem is that the overall level of advertising pollution is increasing, which means that the audiences have become immune and intolerant to the advertising. They are less likely to respond to an ad now then they did years ago. Therefore, it takes more advertising weight to accomplish the same goals. That is, you would have to run many more commercials to the same audience to ensure that the audience is getting your message.

"Despite these challenges, mass media—and, in particular, broadcast (network affiliated) television—is still the most efficient way to deliver an advertising message to a broad audience," according to Brad Baker of Bradford W. Baker (www.BradfordWBaker .com), a media-buying service in Jacksonville, Florida.

The Street Fighter Solution to this dilemma is to discover how to buy your local mass advertising media so that it becomes cost effective for you. This is done in two ways. First, you learn to pay less to reach each one thousand audience members. Second, once you reach them, you deliver a message that will get noticed, remembered, and acted upon.

The possible silver lining in the segmentation of the media is that in some cases it may be easier for a small or niche business to zero in on a specific target audience. Mass media is best at reaching a large percentage of the population. But for most local businesses, a very small subset of that population is a primary target for reaching potential customers.

THE BIG CUT

Cut your media budget in half. With this move, you will not accept having half the media exposure. You have to be a Street Fighter. You will use your wits, knowledge, and guts to make the remaining half of your ad budget do the same job as before the cut. So what do you do with the half you cut? Take 10 per-

> Cut your media budget in half while maintaining the same level of exposure.

cent of it and use it for other proven Street Fighter tactics to supplement your advertising. And with what is left over, go on a vacation, buy a new car, or pay off your student loans. It's your money. You worked hard for it. Don't waste it on advertising that doesn't work.

Linking

One simple way to make a big impact with a small budget is to link your commercial to the content of a given show. Normally, you need to run a commercial repeatedly to make any headway. But if your product or service is the topic of a particular TV show, it takes only a few commercials to get the same results, because the show sells the benefits of the offering. Your commercial simply informs the audience member where to buy the service in your marketplace.

Imagine that you discovered in advance that *Oprah* had an upcoming show on makeovers. Your hair salon, dress boutique, nail salon, makeup counter, weight loss clinic, plastic surgery clinic, or cosmetic dentistry office could promote the same type of service. It may take only a ten-second spot or a brief mention referred to as a "billboard" (not to be confused with an outdoor billboard) to do so. You may have to pay a premium for getting those several "fixed positions" specifically in the show's commercial breaks, but that viewing audience would be more predisposed to buying those services.

The same could be said for marketing cruise lines during reruns of *Love Boat* or an old romantic movie that takes place on a cruise. It would probably *not* work with airings of *Titanic, The Poseidon Adventure* (either version), or the made-for-TV movie about the *Achille Lauro. Gilligan's Island* might be a toss-up.

Certain types of media allow you to present your message in more persuasive ways. A boat dealer can use an odd-size newspaper ad six columns wide (typically thirteen inches) by only two or three inches tall. That short but wide ad is a great dimension for showing off a photo of a boat. Some radio stations and some cable channels can coordinate running your spots to specific circumstances. For example, a heating and air-conditioning dealer (HVAC) wants its radio commercials to run only when the humidity reaches 50 percent or greater or when the temperature exceeds 85 degrees. Those commercials air when the listeners are likely to be in the most discomfort and therefore are predisposed to considering getting help. A car wash runs its commercials only when the prediction is for sunshine for the next two days or longer. Pizza delivery runs commercials more heavily on rainy days when it knows business is likely to pick up. A tire dealer pushes snow tires when there's two or more inches of snow predicted. Auto-body repair shops run their spots when there's ice or hail warnings and other hazardous driving conditions. My karate instructor used to run his advertising on TV when the FBI would come out with its latest statistics on violent crime. His message was marketing self-defense and personal safety.

Brad suggests that before you buy any kind of mass media, you must really understand who your customers are. The more you can identify your customers demographically, psychographically, and geographically, the easier it is to buy media that is most likely to reach them. Making this effort saves you a tremendous amount of money in the long run, while making your advertising a lot more effective.

In addition to going through your database and identifying your clients by zip code, you can also conduct inexpensive surveys. Have an employee call your customers or stand in front of your building with a clipboard and ask them questions as they leave. Find out their pastimes, hobbies, favorite radio stations, TV shows, what kinds of cars they drive, and so on. One quick-oil-change place listed all the major radio stations at the bottom of its worksheet/invoice. While the service attendant was checking the car's odometer, he would also circle the radio station that the radio was tuned to. If he had time, he would even mark off the radio stations that the owner had preprogrammed. This gave the oil-change center an indication which stations its customers listened to.

When Brad Baker was handling media buying for a chain of boat dealers, he discovered that a large percentage of boat owners are also baseball enthusiasts. So, while his client may have had to pay a little premium, on a CPM basis, to buy TV spots during baseball games, it was an efficient buy because this advertising effectively reached the target audience.

This approach saves money because you don't waste it on programming that doesn't reach that audience. It takes fewer total spots, or "advertising weight," to effectively deliver the message to the target group than buying a standard rotation.

A flea market client of Brad's tested a variety of advertising approaches, including TV. To track the results of the advertising, the client compared the normal foot traffic against the days when the advertising ran. The client purchased several inexpensive people counters and had them installed at the only two entrances to the building. These mechanical counters gave the owner an indication which advertising generated the most foot traffic.

Brad recounted a quote he heard early in his career that he feels still applies: "Good advertising is common sense plus applied mathematics." The mathematics, however, is only as good as the numbers you put into the equations.

> Good advertising is common sense plus applied mathematics.

Take a little time to learn about ratings. It's complicated, but a cursory familiarization can be the difference between a money-losing campaign and a moneymaking campaign. Any basic media book will explain ratings.

Your advertising budget is a big variable in your cost of doing business. Most of your expenses are fixed, including your rent, utilities, inventory, taxes, and, to some degree, even your payroll. Your marketing expenses—in particular, your advertising budget—is generally viewed as discretionary. If your sales suddenly tanked, the first thing you would likely cut back on is advertising. Huge chunks of advertising budgets are squandered on hastily executed, poorly planned media buys. Oftentimes, the purchase of advertising is reactive instead of preplanned. Without really knowing how to spend it properly, you're better off taking that money to Vegas and gambling with it, because you'll get about the same odds of seeing a return on it and have a lot more fun.

Gain additional insights about your customers by having your media reps provide you with a Scarborough report for your industry, in your market. Scarborough Research measures the shopping patterns, lifestyles, and media habits of consumers locally, regionally, and nationally; Scarborough measurements detail the lives of American adults. According to its website, www.scarborough.com, Scarborough Research's core services include seventy-five local market studies and a national database. These tools cover 1,700 categories and brands, including comprehensive retail shopping behaviors, lifestyle characteristics, in-depth consumer demographics, and media usage patterns.

CRITICAL MASS

Brad Baker, our marketing guru, stresses a concept that he calls "critical mass." Following this approach requires making sure that you buy enough media in a specific period to do the job. "Anything less than critical mass is a waste of money. If you can't afford enough media to make a difference, then simply save your money and wait till you can afford to get enough." For daily newspapers, never buy less than a quarter-page ad; anything smaller gets lost. For that reason, it's suggested that you don't buy the "awareness builder" program, where you get two columns by two inches a couple of times a week for a year or two. In broadcast, critical mass is around 150 gross rating points (GRPs) per week. If you can afford only 75 GRPs, concentrate your ads into three days. If you can't afford that, bank the money.

Brad warns that when applying the critical mass concept to cable, be sure you understand that the GRPs are based on the CDMA and not the DMA. The CDMA is the cable industry's version of the Neilsen "Dominant Market Area." But unlike a true DMA, the CDMA counts only those households that have cable. This makes your numbers look better than they really are. If you want to compare a cable-TV buy to a broadcast-TV buy, make sure you understand that you're reaching a smaller audience.

KNOW YOUR SQAD

To know if you're getting a fair price for your advertising, compare your CPP (cost per point) for your targeted demographic group against the SQAD[11] rating. The media-cost forecasting source (www.squad.com), formerly known as Spot Quotations And Data, collects real costs for national and local radio and TV stations. A good independent media buyer will subscribe to this service. Consider using one to help you negotiate all these variables and place the media for you. As I like to say, "If you don't know SQAD, then you don't know squat!" These numbers will tell you how much businesses and agencies are actually paying for specific day-parts and specific stations and shows. Again, it's the media equivalent of going to a car dealership with a copy of the dealer invoice in hand and a report on all the discounts and rebates available for a given model.

CUSTOM TV TAGS

The major cable companies are starting to incorporate technology that allows a commercial to be played with a different tag in each zone. Eventually you should be able to buy zoned spots on cable. The advantage is that a number of different dealers or franchisees can buy cable and focus in geographically on a specific area. Currently, you can expect to pay a 30 percent premium for this service, but if you pull your business from that zone only, it is actually cheaper to reach your target audience. If you pull from two or more zones, you're better off buying the entire coverage area.

STICK IT

Daily newspapers can zone as well. One way to generate immediate awareness of your sales event, for example, is with a sticky note on the front page of the paper. There's usually no other advertising on the front page. The sticky note provides maximum readership of a very short, simple message. Plus, it usually can be zoned down to a zip code. It may appear expensive; however, given the ability to target geographically with a high-impact, high-readership device, your ROMI could be very attractive. A downside of this tool is that it requires a longer lead time; typically six to eight weeks.

ON-DEMAND ADS

A service that is just now in its infancy is Navic Networks. Navic's targeted overlays allow advertisers to target groups of viewers using interactive overlays on thirty-second, sixty-second, and long-form advertising. Here is an example: Using a special remote control, a viewer who sees a commercial of interest can receive more information with an on-demand video presentation about that product or service. This is perhaps the first major step toward the actual melding of TV and the internet. With Navic (www .navic.tv), you can actually track your response, too.

OTHER PEOPLE'S AD MONEY

In an effort to rein in the cost of your advertising, one of the best solutions is to get someone else to pay for all or part of your advertising. Co-op advertising provides a lot of opportunities for retailers to get help underwriting their advertising. The amount of co-op advertising available to you from your vendors usually depends on a percentage of the product you buy. The same rules have to apply to all the merchants, as a result of the Robinson-Patman Act. But there are ways to get a bigger allotment of co-op funds.

Most manufactures or distributors have a special fund set aside called MDF, or Market Development Funds. You can approach a vendor's zone manager with a professionally thought-out proposal of how you wish to sell a certain amount of units using a certain advertising campaign. Let's say that you plan to spend $50,000 of advertising to achieve this goal. You want a particular vendor to put up perhaps $25,000 of it, even though you've already used up all your co-op funds. By convincing the regional honcho of the benefits of your plan, you stand a good chance of getting that support. Plus, if you can negotiate a special deal with the media that allows you to buy the promised exposure for less, a greater portion of your outlay will be reimbursed as a percentage.

A variation of the co-op advertising program is done by a local award program, the Consumers' Choice Award. A select group of the best businesses in their respective category agree to buy a license to use the award in their advertising and marketing. As a licensee, they each qualify to participate in a television advertising campaign that announces their win to the area consumers. This is done with a thirty-second "donut" spot, where the middle fifteen seconds is specifically about the licensee's company. The cost of participating is about 30 percent less per rating point than the SQAD rating. That means that they are getting local TV airtime on several network affiliates, one independent, and some cable channels at a greatly reduced rate. Additionally, there are dozens of other businesses also running their spots. The public's awareness of the award campaign increased dramatically as well as for the individual winners. In this situation, a number of seemingly unrelated businesses banded together through a special program. With this collection of businesses, Brad Baker had tremendous leverage with the local media to negotiate the rates. Of course, participation in this type of program is limited to those businesses that win the award. The same program was also done with quarter-page ads in a newspaper insert. The key point is that when TV or the newspaper becomes cost prohibitive, there might be ways to join forces with other noncompetitive businesses to pool enough money to motivate the media to be more flexible.

The last piece of the local advertising media puzzle is your ability to buy it for less. Assuming that you really know your target audience and have a message that will cause them to act, your job now is to get as much exposure to the right people as possible, given your limited budget. For local advertising, Marshall McLuhan had it all wrong when he said, "The medium is the message." The Street Fighter states that the "medium is the *driver* of the message." You don't have to have a superentertaining or funny ad to get results. But you do have to have an ad that appeals to the potential buyer with enough benefits to create interest. The more exposure you get with your message, given the same budget, the greater the potential for a return on your marketing investment.

When you buy radio advertising, after you've negotiated the best deal you think you can get, ask for matching commercials that can run anytime during the broadcast day. Even a spot at 3:00 a.m. will have some listeners. If that spot is free, it can only help you with your ROMI. The worst they can tell you is no. I used to ask for matching overnight spots, which the stations would often agree to. This is the time from midnight to 5:59 a.m. Once a station had agreed to it, I would ask it to "bracket" those spots between 5:00 a.m. and 5:59 a.m. The station usually could air a portion of the ads during that time frame. At 6:00 a.m. begins morning drive, where you'll pay a premium. But at 5:59 a.m., you're still in overnight and paying nothing. The audience size doesn't increase 100-fold in the five or ten minutes before 6:00 a.m., but you will pick up a little bit of extra audience by having your ad run at that time.

Brad recommends that you don't get fixated on buying time on the number-one station in town. Because it's so successful, it will likely be less willing to provide you with a better deal than perhaps the third- or fourth-ranked stations. In most markets, the top-ranked radio station has, at most, 20 percent of the radio listening market. That means you can buy 80 percent of the market by using everyone else if you wanted to. The determining factor of where you should put your money is your cost per thousand (CPM). This is the cost to reach each one thousand listeners in your target audience.

You have to drive all over town to get the best deal on gasoline, but to get the best deal on radio, you only have to make some phone calls. Make sure that you are selecting the radio stations based on the best price to reach your target audience, not on what station *you* listen to. If you're buying for any other reason than a good CPM, you're probably paying too much.

Let's say that your target audience is women 25–54. The number-one rated radio station in town may not be number one for that particular demographic. So look only at the numbers for your target audience. Any audience that you pay for outside of your target is a waste of your money.

Frequency

The other consideration when buying radio time is that you want the audience to hear your spot at least five times. It takes five or more hits before a person will absorb enough of your message to act on it. If a station wants you to pay a certain cost per spot, which will prevent you from getting enough total commercials (frequency), then you need to rethink the buy. Concentrate either on cheaper day-parts or a less expensive station. One or two spots in drive time are a waste of money, regardless of the audience size. There's not enough critical mass to do the job.

> Your audience must hear your message at least five times to be effective.

STATION	WOMEN 25–54	COST PER SPOT	COST PER THOUSAND
Station One	50,000	$75	$1.50
Station Two	25,000	$20	$.80
Station Three	10,000	$11	$1.10
Station Four	5,000	$5	$1.00

In the chart above, four different fictional radio stations are being compared. Station One has the largest total audience in the target, but it is also charging the most to reach each listener.

With a budget of $1,000, you could buy thirteen commercials. That may not be enough repetition to do the job for you. On Station Two, you could buy fifty commercials. The audience is half the size, but you could dominate that group. Using a combination of Stations Two, Three, and Four, you could still reach thirty-five thousand in your target with enough frequency to do the job.

There are other factors as well. Format of the station plays into the mix, as well as one other number called CUME. CUME is the total number of different people who have tuned into that day-part. The audience level, or *average quarter hour,* is how many people are tuned into that station at a point in time. Since you know you need a person to hear your commercial at least five times, you will have a better return on your investment with a station with a more loyal audience than a station with a fickle audience. Look for the relationship between average quarter hour and CUME. The lower the ratio, the less turnover that station has. Less turnover means that you can buy fewer commercials to achieve the same results at a station with a higher turnover.

A weekly newspaper can be an affordable alternative to your daily newspaper. Just because you don't read it doesn't mean your potential customers don't. There are thousands of successful weekly newspapers, so they must be doing something right. It certainly deserves a test. Suburban papers tend to do a great job of reporting on neighborhood news. They are distributed in zones, which means that you can reach a more geographically suitable area. For a fair test, use no less than a half-page ad. Test one zone only at first. And use a strong call to action—preferably with a coupon or a special offer—so that if a reader calls, you can track the results. Ask the publisher for a "new advertiser" or "test market" low price, at least as low as the lowest rate on the rate card. Let the publisher know that if your test works, you'll become a regular advertiser, and remind her that the newspaper will have a great case study it can use to sell to other advertisers.

If you find that the suburban papers work for you, and you work with them on a regular basis, you might also have some leverage to suggest an article about your company, to get some additional free exposure.

The local business journal is a weekly paper that reaches members of the business community. Before using it, however, pay close attention to the CPM compared to the business section of your local daily newspaper. I was considering using a business journal in one Midwestern market. Its circulation was around 15,000, and it claimed a pass-along readership of three times that. The local daily newspaper had a weekday subscription of around 200,000. Since a business section generally gets about 65 percent readership, the readership would have been around 130,000. The cost of a quarter-page ad in the daily was twice that of the weekly business journal. But the CPM was so much lower. Even though the journal zeroed in on the target audience we were looking for, the daily reached much of that same audience plus a lot more. Of course, the only way to know for sure is to test and track both.

Negotiate

Most media will negotiate a better price under the right circumstances. The cost is directly related to supply and demand. If the station has a lot of unsold airtime, or a publication is saddled with unsold space, you're more likely to convince it to give you a special price. For TV, stay away during election times. Politicians eat up a lot of airtime, and the stations are required by the Federal Communications Commission to sell it to politicians at the lowest rate they offer to any other advertiser. Ratings sweeps are also bad times to get deals, as is fall, when the new lineup of mediocre network shows comes out. The bigger your budget, the more the station is generally willing to work with you on pricing.

For radio or TV, use the SQAD ratings of the shows or day-parts as your guide to know what kind of deal you should ask for. If the average SQAD rate is $50 per rating point, you want to ask for half that. But if you get at least a 25 percent discount off the SQAD rate, you're doing well. So in this example, any-thing from $25 to $37 per rating point would be acceptable. If a station is not willing to meet your conditions, go to another station. You can achieve your advertising objectives through a variety of approaches, so look at all the alternatives and associ-ated prices to determine the most cost effective way to go. If the local TV stations won't play ball, check your daily newspaper, radio stations, and cable. Perhaps a combination of several of those media can do the job better, given your budget.

Remnants of an Effective Medium

One way to get a station to want to work with you is if you can provide total flexibility in placing your schedule. A two- to three-week window works pretty well. You leave it up to the sta-tion to run your commercials in the major day-parts (prime, fringe, news, late night, daytime, early morning) on the days it has availabilities. You can even offer to buy up any unsold air-time over a period of time, in certain day-parts, at a specific price per spot. This offer may sound like "I'll buy all unsold spots in the month of May, between 3:00 p.m. and 11:30 p.m. at fifty dollars per spot up to one hundred commercials." But be sure to put a cap on it. This strategy is called buying remnants. The same strategy can also work in print.

If you are already using a certain station or publication, it will not usually allow you to buy in this manner, since you've already set a precedent with your ad buying. This strategy would work better if you want to make a major shift in your advertising. If you usually buy a lot of newspaper ads, the TV stations may be willing to accommodate you because they'll see it as found business.

Brad Baker was able to buy remnants for the Consumers' Choice Award by having the client shift from newspaper to TV and cable. He also was able to find something very special with the cable buy: Cable offered a special sixty-second rate for direct response advertisers. This offer allowed them to buy a sixty-second spot for the price of a thirty-second spot. The client added a strong call to action at the end to qualify for direct response status. Brad had the client create a sixty-second commercial by combining two different thirty-second spots. Additionally, he got the client extra exposure by buying through a regional cable office that had a statewide network. So even though the client really was concerned only with the coverage and ratings in the main marketplace, there was additional exposure at no additional cost. The bottom line of this move was that it cut the cost per point for each of the client's licensees in half, while providing wider coverage absolutely free.

Seasonality

If you have a seasonal business, it is futile to attempt, through advertising, to get people to buy in the off-season. Nobody is going to buy a boat in Michigan in November. The best you can hope to do is extend your season a few weeks on either side of the cycle and perhaps prop it up a little bit at the peak. Advertising when people are not in the market to buy is a waste of money. Extending the sales cycle a little is called "broadening the shoulders" and refers to the bell curve of the sales cycle.

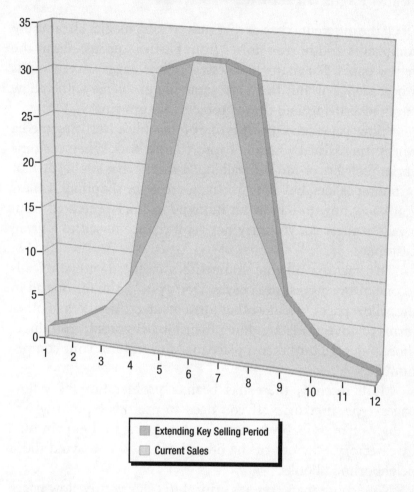

Broaden the Shoulders

No matter what approach you take to your advertising, as stated many times before, it is critical to track your results. Even if you have a campaign that totally bombs, you've learned what not to do in the future. There is always a certain amount of trial and error in advertising. Stick with what works, and dump what doesn't.

Yellow Pages Directories

Of all the different types of mass advertising media, I hear more complaints and horror stories from business people about the yellow pages. For many businesses, yellow pages advertising is a necessary evil. But there are some big problems with yellow pages advertising, and those problems are growing.

Yellow pages advertising is one of the only advertising media where you're listed with all of your competitors. When customers let their fingers do the walking, it means that you'll get a lot of phone callers, but most of them are price shopping. Unless you know how to handle an inbound inquiry generated from a yellow pages ad, you may not get a chance to sell to a given customer.

That fact that all your competitors are listed with you leads to one of my biggest pet peeves. Don't put "Look for our ad in the yellow pages," on any other form of advertising. When other forms of advertising are doing their job, why would you direct those potential buyers to a place that also features your competition?

More recently, there has been a proliferation of yellow pages–type directories. If you need to use this type of advertising, you're probably best serviced by going in the main utility directory. Stay out of the other book, and also avoid those neighborhood books.

Now, more than ever, it's critical to track your yellow pages advertising results. The younger generation, which is very computer savvy, is more likely to search for a supplier, vendor, or service provider via the internet than to schlep out that heavy directory. As this generation ages, this trend may continue to erode the value of your yellow pages advertising.

Ad size is another factor. Yellow pages reps have a reputation for really pushing you to take a bigger ad. If all your major competition has a large ad, you may need one too. But you don't have to be the biggest ad there. You just want a good representation so that buyers know you exist. The trick is to design your ad so that it catches a potential customer's eye. Size alone is not necessary for that.

Treat your yellow pages ad like any other. Don't let the yellow pages rep design it for you. Hire a professional. You are going to have to live with the ad for an entire year, whether it works for you or not. Don't take the chance. Use a strong benefit headline. Make it clear in your ad why you have an advantage over your competition. Also, include a strong call to action. Since color adds to the expense, see if the ad pulls just as many good leads without color.

> A benefit headline is one that tells the audience "what's in it for them."

You may find that if you reduce the size of your ad, the yellow pages people will punish you by moving you deeper into your section. So if you're just starting out, it's best to start small. Test the ad's value. Then, based on the verified results, you can increase the size and test again.

One of my favorite yellow pages stories happened many years ago. In Colorado, there was a small ma-and-pa pizza chain that specialized in delivery. It lived and died by the yellow pages advertising because, back then, if someone wanted a pizza delivered, he looked in the yellow pages under "Pizza." The chain had a small ad that appeared on page 3 of the pizza section, and it worked fine. Then, a few years later, Domino's Pizza started its expansion into this chain's territory. Domino's had a much bigger ad budget and even bought a full-page yellow pages ad. Naturally, Domino's was page 1 in the pizza section. On the back of that ad were four major competitors. And the poor ma-and-pa operation was shoved deeper into the section—so much so, that as soon as the new yellow pages book was published, the ma-and-pa operation's sales dropped dramatically.

What could the owner do? He couldn't compete toe-to-toe with Domino's. But he was a Street Fighter. His solution was to run a campaign that said "Bring us the Domino's yellow pages ad out of the phone book, and I'll give you 2 for 1 pizzas!" People were ripping them out and bringing them in. After that campaign, it was difficult to find a Domino's yellow pages ad anywhere in that market. Domino's was upset; it had to pay for the ad for another eleven months.

Redirect the Number

There is one other example of a creative use of a directory. I was giving a breakout session following my keynote speech for Super 8 Motels at its annual convention in New Orleans. One of the franchisees told me that a big problem it was having was that customers would confuse Super 8 with Motel 6. Many times, customers would call directory assistance and ask for "Motel 8," intending to call Super 8 Motels. More times than not, the operator would tell them that there was no Motel 8, but there *was* a Motel 6. I suggested that they buy a supplemental listing under the name Motel 8. Back then, the cost to add another listing was just about $20 per month. It would be listed in the phone book, but more important, directory assistance would have that listing as well. The phone number, of course, was the same as the local Super 8 Motel. The entire group got very excited about this very simple idea. It might also have been a good idea for them to trademark the name Motel 8 if possible.

That reminds me of the story about a guy who created a long-distance service called "I Don't Know." When a customer was asked by its local service provider which long-distance service he or she wanted, many of the responses were "I don't know." He got all that business.

4

NEIGHBORHOOD MARKETING STRATEGIES
(Taking It to the Streets)

One of the biggest areas of improvement in the ROMI for many small, medium, and even large companies will come from developing and implementing an effective neighborhood level, grassroots marketing program. You usually hear the term *grassroots* used in political campaigns where the supporters literally take their message to the streets. Their minions go door-to-door personally selling their message about a particular candidate. In the business arena, this approach is generally referred to by several terms, including local store marketing, or LSM; neighborhood marketing; and even guerilla marketing.

The potential benefit of such a program has been explored by many organizations, but usually their results fall flat. It sounds goods on paper, but in execution the program falls apart. Therefore, your next Street Fighter Marketing Solution involves an actual plan of attack for developing and implementing a fully integrated local-level marketing program that is designed to work within your organization.

WHAT IS LOCAL-LEVEL MARKETING?

A local-level marketing program is a local-business outreach initiative where owners, managers, and employees who work at an individual location entice the local area consumers to be regular customers. The focus is on the neighborhood or community, that geographic primary trading area from which the majority of customers come. It could include a three- to five-mile radius, or it could be bigger or smaller, depending on the type of business and marketplace. At this level, the mass media is cost prohibitive on an individual unit basis. Even when combining a number of units in a marketplace, the individual local-store marketing approach, when done properly, always shows the highest return for your marketing investment.

The tactics are many, but not all of them work for every situation. Your goal is to collect a war chest of ideas that will allow you to take advantage of the hundreds of opportunities that exist to infiltrate your local area with low-cost and even free advertising designed to generate both initial-trial and repeat sales. But more important than the war chest of tactics, you need a system in place in your organization to ensure proper execution. The tactics are developed for and executed by the individual unit. However, if your company has one hundred franchisees, five hundred dealers, or seventy-five agencies, you also need to create a local marketing infrastructure to support that effort. Most local marketing programs fail, not because of a lack of ideas but because of a lack of follow-through and support. So in addition to many of the specific promotions, it's important to develop and execute an implementation infrastructure that allows you to consistently conduct local marketing programs over time.

> Ideas are easy.
>
> Execution is hard.

HOW ARE STREET FIGHTER MARKETING SOLUTIONS DIFFERENT?

The main emphasis is not on marketing, which is the easiest part of the program. The focus is on training and development. When most local marketing programs get started, the unit manager or owner is usually handed a manual and told to go out into the community and bump up sales. Even a full-day seminar is not enough to give most unit owners or managers the knowledge and skills needed to implement the programs. Think of it like the military. You wouldn't hand someone a gun and a helmet, point to the battlefield, and tell him to engage the enemy. Soldiers are well trained. It's unfair to expect an operations-focused person to develop marketing and sales skills on his own. Soldiers go through boot camp, specialty training, on-the-job training, certification, and so on. A similar approach is needed to make your Street Fighter Marketing program work.

Even with the expense of the training program, the ROMI is still high, because once you've developed the program and trained your local managers, you have an asset that keeps on performing for you for many years to come. Even with an acceptable amount of turnover, you'll find that your ROMI is very attractive.

WHY LOCAL MARKETING?

Local marketing is literally the missing link for most major marketing strategies. This strategy is well suited for large companies whose primary method of distribution is through their local dealer, agency, or franchisee network. Consider a major company like Goodyear Tire and Rubber Company. One of its primary distribution channels is through the five thousand independent Goodyear dealerships. Though each store may carry some competing brands, Goodyear is each one's primary tire vendor. Those dealers attend Goodyear meetings and go to Goodyear conventions. They get Goodyear co-op advertising dollars and floor displays. And, at some time in a store's history, its owner might even get a ride on one of the three Goodyear blimps.

Those five thousand stores serve five thousand different neighborhood communities. Local marketing perfectly supplements the national advertising Goodyear does to promote its brand and the marketwide advertising that it does to promote all the Goodyear stores in a given television viewing area (DMA or ADI).[12] The single dealer may wonder what he can do in his community to bring in more business. He's on a limited budget, runs his own operation, and is trained mostly in the area of the automotive aftermarket. Mostly, the dealers buy local newspaper advertising, which features price and items. And there's nothing more exciting to the customer than to find out how to get a deal on a set of P205/65 R15s!

Now, imagine if there was a program where a significant number of those five thousand independent dealers aggressively promoted Goodyear to their neighborhoods *consistently* over the years. That could sell a lot more tires, and the cost of those additional sales would be a fraction of what it would cost to generate those sales through the mass media.

While the concept is very simple, the execution is very involved. It's well worth the effort because the end result is that all the national, regional, and marketwide advertising Goodyear does becomes dramatically more effective. The dealer trained in Street Fighter Solutions is more readily able to convert those mass media gross rating points and race-car sponsorships into more and more sales.

The same tactics can be used by local businesses of any size, whether or not mass media is an option. From the appropriate Fortune 500 to the ma-and-pa, this approach will work. It's also beneficial to the regional and local players. It doesn't matter if the company has five thousand locations, five hundred, fifty, or five; the same tactics apply.

With Street Fighter neighborhood marketing, all players compete on a somewhat level playing field. Of course, those local businesses that have the benefit of multiple locations and of national and regional advertising to promote their brand still hold an advantage. Nonetheless, a local independent can go head-to-head. Several years ago, Burger King launched an ill-fated advertising campaign to take on McDonald's in the so-called "burger wars." The problem was that Burger King couldn't begin to challenge McDonald's because McDonald's simply had significantly more assets. It had twice as many locations and a significantly larger advertising budget. The way to beat McDonald's was not in a big national campaign. It was through the equivalent of a marketing insurgency. First, Burger King should have planned a successful branding campaign with the bulk of its national advertising dollars. Then, with a small fraction of that money and a good plan, it should have developed and executed an effective, comprehensive local neighborhood program. To do this right at that level, it would have taken at least two years—perhaps as much as three years. But at that end of that time, Burger King would have had a stealth program that would have allowed individual stores to effectively compete against all of their top rivals on an individual unit basis. Plus, once developed, it would have required a very small amount of money to maintain.

Local-level marketing isn't for every business. It might not be as applicable for businesses whose products or services don't reach the consumer directly. It's also less effective for operations that don't pull most of their sales from the immediate neighborhood. This may include big-box retailers such as Wal-Mart, Home Depot, and OfficeMax. But it would apply to the local businesses that are often hurt when these big-box retailers come to town.

WHO IMPLEMENTS LOCAL-LEVEL MARKETING?

To be most effective, local-level marketing tactics need to be executed by the person running the local unit. That could be the manager or owner—whoever runs the unit on a daily basis. It doesn't matter if it's the ma-and-pa owner of the store, or the franchisee, or the manager that works for the major corporation, as long as execution comes from the local level. Of course, this raises concerns for many operationally focused businesses. They want their managers running their stores and not marketing. That's a mistake. Some organizations want to hire a special person to conduct the local marketing, usually for several stores. That's also a mistake.

It is critical that your local manager conduct the local-level marketing program, for several reasons. First, if you have to pay someone to do it for you, it is no longer cost effective. Second, to take advantage of the hundreds of low-cost local promotional opportunities, you have to be totally immersed in the local community. An outside person, who swings in once every couple of weeks and is responsible for a number of neighborhoods, just can't have that kind of awareness and community access. Third, as these types of programs start to develop awareness among members of a community over time, the local manager becomes known. This local notoriety can be leveraged to create even more effective local marketing.

> For maximum ROMI, execution must come from the owner or manager of the local store.

MOST COMMON MISTAKES

1. Not allowing enough time to fully develop the program:
The developmental phase allows you to provide the rest of your stores with a program that is much easier to implement and more likely to be successful sooner. Cutting the development phase too soon short-circuits that effort.

2. Expecting franchisees to implement without training and support:
Many times, a local marketing program begins and ends with a manual and/or a seminar. These are tools that help kick off such a program, but it's the follow-up process that makes it successful. Remember, you are dealing with elements of adult learning and behavior modification.

3. Not providing enough support from above:
All levels of management must support a successful local marketing program just as if introducing a new product, equipment, or procedure. Even the highest levels of management can help by letting the rank and file know how much the local marketing program can mean to the company's overall success.

4. Not allowing the one-on-one marketing element to happen:
Some organizations are concerned that allowing franchisees or store managers to do some marketing will interfere with their operations. Therefore they want to bring in an army of local marketing people to do it for them. This is too costly and ineffective. The store franchisee is in a unique position to have his finger on the pulse of the community. This is the first step in dominating the neighborhood.

5. Trying to make it more complicated than it needs to be:
When the local marketing program is developed by an
advertising agency or marketing group without specific local
marketing experience, it focuses on the tactics, ideas, manual,
and so on. These firms have a tendency to suggest ideas that
are impractical for an overworked, overstressed franchisee or
store manager.

6. Having unrealistic expectations:
Local marketing works only in stores that have solid operations
and good customer service. An effective local marketing
program will run a bad operation out of business faster. But if
awareness and trial are the problems, local marketing can be
very effective.

7. Expecting a short time horizon:
Local marketing is not an overnight program. Traceable results
are slow in coming but easily sustainable. The cost per new
customer is much lower than any other form of marketing
except for direct referral.

The Big McStake

When big companies try to implement a local-store marketing
program, they always seem to fall flat. The reason is that local
marketing is so different from any other programs that they've
tried to implement in the past. Most efforts usually consist of
a manual developed by a company's advertising agency. An ad
agency has no idea how to make local marketing work. That's not
its expertise. The manual ends up on the shelf gathering dust. The
process that you will use to develop and implement a powerful
local marketing program will parallel the way that most organizations introduce a new product or service to the marketplace.

PHASE ONE

Step One: Local Marketing Audit

Before reinventing the wheel, take a look at some of the local promotions that your people are already doing. See what is getting results and fully understand how those promotions work. You'll also uncover some less successful promotions. Understanding these will help you from making the same mistakes that have already been made. Get the stories behind the promotions. Find out what the specific problem was or what opportunity this promotion

> This is *not* a test.
> This is a development program.

was geared to help with. Collect the real numbers when possible. If someone says the promotion was successful, get proof. How many new customers did it generate? How many additional sales did it generate? How have sales overall been affected by the promotion? What were the real costs in both time and money to execute it?

Step Two: Developmental Market and Unit Selection

Select several markets with several units each. The size of the developmental group will depend on the overall size of your company, but it should generally consist of about 5 percent to 10 percent of your company's total number of units, as long as it is no greater than 50 units (for larger companies) or less than 5 units (for small companies). From a cost-savings standpoint, it helps to select markets where there is a concentration of good units.

In each developmental market, you'll choose between five and ten stores that are already successful. You don't want any stores participating in this phase that are unprofitable or poorly managed. You may get pressure from upper management to use this program to save the losers. However, this is the wrong time to work on those units. That will come later.

Your immediate challenge in the development phase is to beta test "generic" promotional ideas. Execution of these ideas converts generic tactics to promotions proven to work specifically for your organization. Using low-volume stores is a bad idea, because low-volume stores will be a detriment to your development. You'll spend much more of your resources to get a loser to break even than you will to get a successful store to increase its volume by the same amount. Plus, the equivalent percentage growth in a good store is a lot more profitable to the overall system.

At the same time, be careful about including stores that are *too* successful. The managers of those stores might be less cooperative with the program, since they're already showing good numbers. Though there are exceptions, your best bet is to select a group of stores that are in the top half to top third in volume, but be cautious with the top 5 percent to 10 percent. You also want to make sure that the managers of those locations really support the program.

Step Three: The Initial Training Seminar

You teach your developmental group the basic Street Fighter tactics in a half-day or full-day seminar. You can do this either once in each market or bring them all together in one location if the expenses look better. Some of these tactics are presented in the next several chapters. The manual that you create is for training and reinforcement only. The seminar leader takes each participant through the process, using role playing to get these managers and owners used to executing the promotions. At the same time, the supervisory level people (area supervisors, district managers, among others) are also learning the program.

Step Four: Supervised In-field Execution

Immediately following the seminar, you visit each participating unit and coach the manager or owner individually, one-on-one, through his first few promotions. You even set up the first promotion together. Leave nothing to chance. This is a critical step because it helps the manager get past his initial discomfort in setting up these types of programs. Once a manager experiences how easy it is, you have a much better chance of getting him fully involved in the program.

Step Five: Weekly Support

Once a week, you have an individual telephone training session with each participant. In that phone session, you review what happened the previous week. If there were glitches, you help the participant work on it. Then you help the participant set specific goals for the next week. In this way, you'll know weekly if the programs are getting done. Immediately follow the telephone session with a memo or email summarizing the conversation. Send it to the participant, the supervisor, and as many people up the chain of command that want to keep an eye on the program. It's these summaries that will become the bulk of your fully customized version of the program when you're ready to roll it out systemwide.

Step Six: Monthly Review, Revise, and Recharge (R^3) Group Sessions

Monthly, bring the local participants together in their market for a review and advanced Street Fighter training. This step can be done by telephone conference, but it is vastly more effective if the participants can meet in person. In these sessions, each participant shares with the rest of the group what he has done and how each promotion worked or didn't work. We find that this process accelerates the program because peers sharing success stories creates enthusiasm for the program. It also puts subtle pressure on those that are lackluster in their efforts. You serve more as a facilitator than anything in these sessions.

Immediately following these group training sessions, compose a memo or email summarizing the activity and issues. Then send it to all the participants and their supervisors.

Ideally, you want to continue on this course for no less than six months and upward of twelve. Using a full year for development allows you to include examples of various seasonal and holiday promotions. Toward the end of this developmental phase, you should have collected enough tactical stats, samples, and stories to start the next phase of the program.

As mentioned before, this is the most difficult phase, as far as implementation and getting overall results from specific promotions. These developmental groups are being trained in a generic version of the program, and it is through their efforts that the program becomes customized for your entire system. The program that is presented in the rollout seminar will be far more effective that the one that was presented six to twelve months earlier because all the ideas will have been fine-tuned during that first phase. It amazes me, when I'm conducting a generic Street Fighter seminar at a convention: I'll teach one tactic and share a supporting anecdote of a pizza place that used it successfully. An audience member may run a car wash and say, "That's fine for pizzas, but how does that work for me?" As incredible as it may seem, the majority of your managers won't be able run with a given tactic unless it is presented step-by-step, specifically for the business they run.

During the development phase, you'll also collect numerous samples of printed pieces that were used in the promotions. These certificates, coupons, flyers, danglers, shelf talkers, mailers, and so on will have been produced for each specific promotion. From these, you will then create templates that are easy to customize for all other future participants. Some businesses will keep the templates on file through their local quick-printing service so that that managers or owners can easily go online, add their contact information, adjust the offer and disclaimers, and then have them printed and delivered.

In addition to local implementation of the various promotions, it's usually beneficial to allow your unit managers to order their own print materials from their local vendors. Of course, you will want to use preapproved templates or camera-ready ad slicks to ensure that they are following your programs and including all the necessary legal disclaimers, but your local managers need the ability to arrange for their promotional pieces locally. If you force them to deal with a centralized service, either externally or internally, it will frustrate them, and the program will be at risk of falling apart. The additional cost of printing is so minimal that it's not worth taking the chance.

One very good way to help the corporation with the support and control of the local marketing materials is with an online solution called The Agilis Marketing Suite from Saepio Technologies (www.saepio.com). With Agilis, you have complete control of your branding while enabling your local unit operators to easily customize, produce, and order locally relevant content for your print, broadcast, and digital applications. Your franchisees, managers, or dealers can use a standard web browser to customize all of your print advertising, including flyers, cross promotion pieces, direct mailers, and so on. It even allows you to have an e-commerce function that allows materials to be purchased on line. It also allows you to distribute and customize radio, video, and direct mail lists.

Step Seven: Step-down Phase

Once you're comfortable that your participants are regularly implementing their Street Fighter tactics, you begin to wean them off the weekly calls and monthly meetings. I suggest that first you go from weekly phone calls to one call every two weeks and one meeting every other month. After three months of that, you'll then reduce to one call every three weeks and one meeting every three months. Then, finally, call once a month and have a group meeting once every four to six months. This will be the maintenance level you stay with forever. The step-down process, which begins as you start phase two, is important for maintaining the program; if you stop "cold turkey," you stand a chance of losing all the momentum you've built in the previous six to twelve months of your program.

Your developmental markets will also begin to provide you some advanced tactics that only happen in the more mature Street Fighter Marketing units. These improvements, modifications, and innovations can happen only if you keep the program going in the original developmental markets. They will provide you with much of the new material that you'll use in all the other markets after the rollout phase.

The Dirty Dozen II

Once you determine the optimum number of participating units to develop your program, you'll want to start with a few extras. We call this the Dirty Dozen approach. In *The Dirty Dozen: The Next Mission*, Lee Marvin chooses thirteen prisoners who are either on death row or long sentences to go on a mission. If they survive, their sentences will be commuted. However, if a prisoner gets out of line just once, he is sent back for immediate execution of his sentence. During the first day of training, one of the prisoners tries to cause

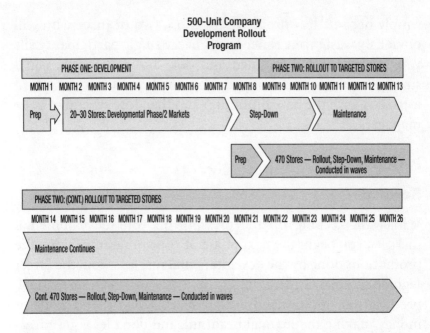

500-Unit Company
Development Rollout
Program

Figure 1 The flowchart shows how the development phase evolves into the rollout phase of the program on a month-by-month basis.

trouble. He is immediately shipped back. The remaining twelve clean up their act instantly.

We know from experience that not everyone is going to do well in this first phase. Keep in mind that in the development phase, you're using generic tactics. It's going to be more difficult to show results than it will be in phase two, which occurs when all the ideas have been flushed out. Therefore, if you need, let's say, twenty-five units for nine months to develop your program properly, you'll actually start with 10 percent more, or twenty-eight units. You usually can't tell prior to beginning who is going to be a superstar and who is going to be a super pain in the rear, but you'll discover it within the first few weeks. There is also the natural attrition that happens when employees move or quit. Don't make a big deal of it. You simply become less proactive for those two or three who will obviously waste your time. And if every single participant calls you weekly when scheduled and does his homework, you'll simply have a more developed program. What you can't afford is to start with the bare minimum and then lose several of your managers.

PHASE TWO

Rewrite

While still keeping up the pressure on your developmental markets, you begin the next phase of your program. Taking the promotions done by the developmental markets, you, the Street Fighter seminar leader, will create a new participant manual, presentation outline, and audiovisuals. Don't spend a lot of money making the manual beautiful, and don't let your advertising agency produce it for you. With any luck, it will be obsolete within six months. The reason is because we assume that you'll have numerous improvements and innovations to share with future managers.

Rollout

With the new presentation materials, you start to plan your rollout process. This process, in some respects, will follow the way a new product or procedure is rolled out. You'll choose some key markets to start with. You will want markets that are already reasonably successful. You'll save your worst markets for a little later, when you're better equipped to turn them around.

Unlike introducing a new product through a national advertising campaign, you will roll out your Street Fighter local marketing program more slowly and methodically. Pick your rollout markets carefully. You'll include all the units within those markets, but you can be selective in assigning weekly phone calls to only those units that are really going to support the program.

The number of units a Street Fighter trainer can handle during the rollout phase will depend on several factors. The key is to concentrate units in a marketplace. Since you'll have to conduct a monthly meeting with all the participants, you'll want to choose locations that a number of unit managers or owners can get to easily. Generally, a three-hour drive or less works well, although we have had areas where managers came longer distances. If your participants are scattered all over the place, facilitating the process is more difficult. In those situations, we have done some of the meetings by conference call or in a webinar (online seminar)format. The problem is that these types of meetings don't have the same power as meeting in person.

Next you will consider the total number of participants. Each participant requires a ten- to fifteen-minute phone call per week. Not all of them will call you when they're supposed to, and you'll have to be proactive to reach them, taking more of your time. Then, for each phone call, you will have write a summary memo afterward, which will take another five to ten minutes.

Once you start the step-down portion of the rollout in a given market, you'll find that you have more time available to start a new market. You may be tempted (or feel pressure from your bosses) to speed up this process, but speeding up things will trade off some of the maximum benefit from the program. With enough trainers, you can conduct an effective rollout in a twelve-to-eighteen-month period.

Turnarounds

When the bulk of your units are in maintenance, or starting their step-down process, you can then focus on the problem

LSM PROGRAM—TWELVE MONTHS AT A GLANCE

PHASE I: DEVELOPMENT

1. Month One (Predevelopment)
a. Choose participating markets and stores.
b. Field research to prepare initial kickoff seminar.
c. Phone interviews of franchisees.
d. Prepare seminar outline.
e. Prepare approved promotional pieces.

2. Month Two (Kickoff)
a. Kickoff seminar.
    i. Conducted in each participating market.
    ii. Half-day, interactive.
    iii. Leave with plan of attack.
b. Store visits.
c. Weekly phone calls.

3. Months Three–Eleven
a. Monthly half-day group training sessions.
    i. Review activities.
b. Weekly phone calls.
    i. Review previous week's efforts.
    ii. Agree on specific tasks for following week.
    iii. Address unique problems and opportunities.
c. Weekly review emails/notes.
    i. Copies to management.
d. Open 800 number hotline for problems/opportunities.
    i. 800-SLUTSKY.

4. Month Twelve (Pre-rollout)
a. Create totally customized seminar and program.
    i. Procedures outline for initiating a new market/unit.
    ii. Custom seminar workbook/manual.
    iii. Seminar outline.
        1. Incorporate all statistics, anecdotes, procedures.
        2. Create camera-ready art and preapproved offers.
    iv. Consider an LSM reinforcement campaign.
        1. Newsletter.
        2. E-zine.
        3. Conference call.
b. Place initial participants in maintenance mode.
    i. Group sessions quarterly.
    ii. Conference call quarterly.
    iii. Weekly phone calls and tracking.

units. Before investing your valuable resources in these financially challenged units, it helps to first determine the reason why they are underperforming.

Marketing, advertising, and promotion can't help a poorly managed unit. It can't help a unit that is in poor repair. It will have minimal benefit for a poorly located unit. So, it's advised that you correct these operational and managerial problems before instituting the Street Fighter program.

Assuming there are no operational reasons why a unit is an underachiever, you're now ready to resuscitate it. It's likely that the unit will have a poor reputation in the marketplace, even though the problems have been fixed. For these units, you'll conduct a more intensive series of promotions designed to put it back on the map fast. Again, these tactics are discussed in the next chapters. The process you will use to install your Street Fighter program is similar to the rollout process; however, it is more intensive.

MAINTENANCE PHASE

This final phase is critical and often forgotten. Without some consistent effort to reinforce the program, it's too easy for store managers to lapse into old habits, and all that hard work will be for nought. It doesn't take a lot to maintain the program. There should be some kind of live event once a quarter. That could be a phone call, conference call, group meeting in a specific market, or a regional or national Street Fighter Marketing convention. Plus, you want to supplement the live events with other reinforcements, such as a newsletter, an e-zine, emails, video updates on the company website, and so on.

Your Street Fighter program becomes part of the daily operation. For that reason, I like to call this an operations-based marketing program. It should take only five or ten minutes daily to maintain the program once you've reached this level. Your area supervisors and district managers need to learn how to manage the program as part of their operational oversight duties. They will also be able to set up promotions from time to time that are executed on a marketwide or regional basis.

Recognition for a manager or owner's efforts is also important. When your organization starts rewarding local marketing programs, the unit managers will understand how important their efforts are to the company. For maximum motivation, not only present awards for successes, but make it part of their bonus program as well.

Special Forces

Your last step is to address the special needs of the different units. You need a "what if?" program in place. Some of these special needs might include: the grand opening of a new store; a store remodeling; competitive intrusion; competitive exit; a managerial change; and access barriers, such as a road widening in front of the store or storm damage.

Replacement

You need a way to train new managers. Either through expansion or attrition, you will lose some of your trained Street Fighters. New ones will take their place. So part of your maintenance program is to bring the new managers online. You could have Street Fighter training form part of the standard operations training.

One other thing you'll want to explore is building your Street Fighter team. To do all this stuff, you'll need enough of the right people to make it happen. Of course, the number of people needed depends on the size of your organization. Keep in mind that as the program grows, so does the cost. For each person that you add to your staff to exclusively work on Street Fighter programs, you must show an increase in sales to justify the addition. Work smarter, not harder. Keep your team lean and mean. After all, they're Street Fighters.

In the next chapter, you'll explore some of the actual tactics.

5

NEIGHBORHOOD MARKETING TACTICS (Doing It in the Streets)

With your Street Fighter neighborhood marketing infrastructure in place, you're ready to start making some tactical headway. Obviously, not every tactic is appropriate for every business or situation. In this chapter, you will learn a variety of Street Fighter tactics. If at first one of these tactics doesn't seem to apply to your situation, try to adapt, modify, enhance, or otherwise tweak it. Sometimes the most successful promotions are adaptations of other ideas that, on the surface, didn't seem to apply. As a Street Fighter, you learn how to identify successful ideas used elsewhere and then make them work for you. We call this "creative borrowing."

In some respects, the tactics presented here are like a wedding: something old, something new, something borrowed, and something blue. The honeymoon is usually over after the first few months of the program. But by then your efforts should prove fruitful.

BUSINESS CARDS

To demonstrate just how simple a successful promotion can be, here are some examples executed with nothing but simple business cards.

Treading for Business

A tire dealer is constantly looking for business opportunities. While out, if he happens to notice that a car has balding tires, he leaves a special business card on the windshield that says, "I happened to notice that your tires are in bad shape. This card is good for a 10 percent savings on a new set."

Free Cup of Coffee Creates New Customers

Barbara is the manager of a convenience store in Parkersburg, West Virginia. During an eleven-week period when she would be away from the store, she passed out 200 of her business cards to people she did not recognize as being her customers. She made a goal of handing out at least 10 a day. On the back of her business card, she would write "free regular soft drink or coffee," and sign it. Then she would tell people to whom she handed cards that the soft drink was on her if they came into her convenience store. Of the 200 that she passed out, 51 cards were brought back, for over a 25 percent return. Obviously, most of those people who came in and redeemed that card bought other things. Plus, many of those customers came back for more visits.

Hindsight Promotion

A very successful stockbroker on the East Coast used a different version of business card distribution, according to Murray

Raphael, coauthor of *The Great Brain Robbery*. While commuting to work, this stockbroker would have to pay several tolls. Before he paid his tolls, he would first look in his rearview mirror. If he saw an upscale car, he would pay not only his toll but also the toll of the person in the luxury car behind him. He would then ask the toll booth attendant to hand his business card to the person in the car behind him. On the back, he'd written: "If you think this is an interesting way of getting your attention, think of all the things I could do for your financial portfolio." He got many new clients from a simple ninety-cent toll and clever use of his business card.

The Business Card Drawing

When we're brought into an organization to develop and help implement a Street Fighter Marketing program, the first tactic we get participating managers to use is the business card drawing. In the hands of a Street Fighter, this simple tactic provides several key pieces of information that can be used in executing many promotions over the following six to twelve months.

The business card drawing helps you conduct a little bit of reconnaissance about your marketplace, so that you will get maximum return on your efforts. Knowing in which parts of town your customers live and work can be a real advantage when developing special promotions. Or, more to the point, knowing what areas of your neighborhood don't seem to patronize you is equally as important.

No doubt you've seen fishbowls in businesses for dropping in your business card for a free drawing. You'll do the same, but you're going to use the promotion for more than just creating a mailing list. On the poster above the fishbowl, specifically make the drawing a business card–only drawing. You don't provide entry forms. The reason is that the business card provides you with information that you will want later. Plus, for this pro-motion, you want to gather the names of business people who happen to be your customers. Of course, if you have a customer that doesn't have a business card and wants to participate in the drawing, you can have him write his name and address on a piece of paper or on the back of your card. The prize you select for your free drawing should be just valuable enough to motivate custom-ers to enter. You don't want to it to be so valuable that people want to "stuff" your fishbowl. Also, mention on the contest sign that runner-up prizes will also be awarded.

Pushpin Chart

After several weeks, you'll draw a winner and give away your prize. You will be left with a fishbowl full of business cards. The infor-mation on these cards is invaluable. First, the cards tell you where your customers work. So your first task is to do a scattergram. A scattergram is made from a street map of the trade area around your business. Plot the addresses on the map with pins with col-ored heads. Once you start plotting enough of your customers on the map, you begin to get a picture of where your customers work. You might be pleasantly surprised where you get business.

Once you have your map plotted, take a step back and see exactly where your customers work. With this information, you can plan an attack for those geographical areas where you have a weak concentration. For example, if the reason a certain area draws few customers is because there is a park or a lake located there, then you know nothing can be done. However, if the map shows a very weak pull from an area where you have stiff com-petition, you'll want to attack that area with aggressive promo-tional offers.

The scattergram can also be used to plot home addresses; however, for that piece of recon, you will need to provide entry forms and ask for home addresses. Do not run both drawings at the same time.

A scattergram can also be useful to help you select local advertising media. Brad Baker uses the scattergram to determine which local newspapers to buy ads in for his clients. When the daily newspaper has too broad a reach and is therefore too expensive for a given local businessperson, there are suburban and other weekly publications that may do the job. Brad uses the scattergram information to "determine geographically which publications reach the customers."

The Database

The obvious benefit, as mentioned before, is using the information you gathered to build your database. You can use the addresses for mailings, the phone numbers for calling, and the fax numbers for broadcast faxing. Since they're already your customers, you can ask if they would like to get on your "hot list" (preferred customer list or VIP list) so that when you have special offers, you can give them prior notice before your ad breaks in the newspaper.

Cross-promotion Partner Leads

The biggest challenge in neighborhood marketing is having the time to meet with other area merchants to set up various cross-promotions. Over the years, this was the one big drawback to getting the ideas implemented. I was challenged by a client, a major quick-oil-change franchisor, to come up with a way for an overworked store manager to set up these promotions, given the demands on his time already. The answer was sitting in the waiting room.

I was working with one of several managers in the development phase of their program on the West Coast. I noticed a gentleman in a very nice suit reading a four-month-old copy of *Time* magazine while waiting for his car. We started chatting. It turned out that he was a recent transfer to the area and headed the human resources department for the John Deere distribution center about a mile down the road. This was his second visit to the store after bringing in his wife's car the week before. He was really pleased with the quality of service. I asked him if he would like to provide his three hundred employees a new benefit program at no cost to his company. That got his attention.

I then offered to provide special VIP cards that allowed all of his employees to receive a 10 percent discount on any oil change for a three-month period. The only caveat was that the piece had to be inserted in the payroll envelope in order to ensure that every employee received one. The VIP cards would be printed specifically for them and have the John Deere name on the card and say that this is a new employee benefit. He thought this was a great idea, and the promotion was executed.

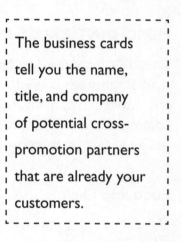

The business cards tell you the name, title, and company of potential cross-promotion partners that are already your customers.

We had been teaching our participants how to set up these types of promotions for years, but this one was different. The promotion was set up on-site. I did not have to go knocking on any doors. The time saved was enormous. Plus, the decision maker in this case was already a customer. He needed no introduction to the business, so he was predisposed to working with my client.

That's where your business card drawing comes in. These cards tell you the names of the companies and the titles of the people who are already your customers. Like the John Deere example, you can likely set up your first twenty or thirty promotions with your own customers. Your customer database is your secret weapon to making this work for you.

The more you know about your own customers, the more opportunities you'll have to promote. Business card drawing aside, you'll also use this approach to develop nonprofit fundraising opportunities as well, which are designed to bring customers into your location. Starting with your own customer base as a means to create your community outreach program is the key to success.

MERCHANT CROSS-PROMOTION

The VIP card idea is just one type of cross-promotion. That particular approach is used when networking with major employers, educational institutions, and other associations in your community. A similar promotion executed a little differently is designed for you to network with other area merchants.

Food and Flicks

Steve is the unit manager of a Back Yard Burgers restaurant in Tennessee mentioned in an earlier chapter. One of his regular customers is the assistant manager of a Blockbuster video store in his neighborhood. One day Steve sat down with the guy while he was having lunch at the restaurant and had a free dessert brought to him. He told the Blockbuster assistant manager that he had this idea he wanted to run by him. Back Yard Burgers had just introduced four new desserts (one of which had just been given to the customer). Once Steve saw that the assistant manager liked the dessert, he said that he'd like to offer each Blockbuster customer a free dessert. There was interest, so Steve gave his customer the details of his idea. For one weekend, each Blockbuster customer would receive a special certificate for a free dessert with any burger purchase. Steve presented it as a way for Blockbuster to show its appreciation to its customers.

In just the first few weeks of the promotion, Steve generated ninety-two *new* customers. To determine if a customer was a first-timer, Steve had his counter people ask each customer with the certificate if it was his or her first time to this Back Yard Burgers. This simple question helped to differentiate a new customer from a regular. That number no doubt increased over the following weeks. Oddly enough, BYB received an additional fifty-five redemptions at one of the restaurant's other locations farther away.

In this situation, Steve already knew the customer. What made the promotion a Street Fighter Solution was that Steve set it up in several minutes and without leaving the store. It showed not only a tremendous return on his financial investment, but saved time.

The business card drawing will help you to find more of these types of opportunities. However, if you can jot down the names of customers that you already know and who would make ideal cross-promotion partners for you, start there. If you don't want to wait for those key customers to come in, use the phone number on the business card and invite them in. Tell them that you had your drawing, and they won the runner-up prize. Set a specific time for the customer to come pick it up or ask when he or she plans on visiting again, so that you can make sure the prize is ready. When that person comes in is when you suggest your idea for a promotion.

You shouldn't have to leave your unit to set up a number of promotions over time, as mentioned before. However, there are times when a promotion's ROMI can be potentially so huge that you want to take the time to go to them.

Such was the situation with Jason, the manager of a Mid-western comic-book store. His product, unlike burgers or video rentals, appeals to a very small percentage of the marketplace. Finding a cross-promotion partner that would be worth the effort was not easy until the release of the first *Batman* movie sequel. Jason reasoned that not everyone who would go to this movie buys comic books, but just about everyone who buys comic books would go to this movie. There are not very many venues where he could potentially reach nearly 100 percent of his potential buyers.

So Jason set up a promotion with a movie theater during the release of *Batman Returns*. With each ticket sold, the moviegoer got a certificate for $1 off the purchase of any $10 worth of Batman products. The movie theater handed out 10,000 certificates. The raw exposure alone had some value, yet even better, the comic book store got 150 redemptions. Out of that, 50 became regular customers, spending an average of $10 per week in the store. It generated about $26,000 of yearly revenue on a onetime $100 promotion! That was certainly worth the extra effort. Plus, once the relationship was established, Jason could return for the release of other similar title-specific opportunities, including *Superman, Spider-Man, X-Men, Fantastic 4, The Punisher, Catwoman,* and so on.

The Three Cs

To be fair, not all cross-promotions have this dramatic a result. Still, when done right, why does this type of cross-promotion offer such a high return on investment? To understand, let's look at the three Cs of cross-promotion:

1. Cost
2. Control
3. Credibility

Cost

The most expensive thing about any advertising is the cost of getting your message distributed to your potential customers. When you buy radio, you pay for the number of people listening. When you buy newspaper, you pay for the number of subscribers reading. With a cross-promotion, on the other hand, you get free distribution of your advertising message. Even the cost of production is minimal. You don't have to use full color and special paper. Simple black ink on standard color-paper stock works fine at your local quick printer.

Control

With a cross-promotion, you get the same control as you would with direct mail. You can target geographically and demographically to reach just the people you want to reach. In Jason's situation, he figured that people who went to a movie based on a comic book character would be an ideal group to promote to. And he was right. In Steve's situation, he was able to find a high-volume business geographically situated to help him.

There's one other interesting play with "geographic control." If, after completing your scattergram, you discover that you have weak pull from a certain area because a major competitor is located there, you can plan some surgical attacks. Set up promotions specifically around that competitor. You'll probably have to use a stronger offer or deeper discount to pull customers to you because they are farther away, and there's a competitor between you. You will probably get less return than usual, but the customers you do pull are more likely to be new.

Geographic control also means that you think very carefully about the businesses with whom you cross-promote in relation to their distances from your business. One of our earlier efforts involved a Minit-Lube manager who set up a cross-promotion with the Dairy Queen right next door. People came in to get their oil changed and since they had a few minutes to kill, the Diary Queen advertisement for "99¢ Peanut Buster Parfaits" on the reader board was just too tempting. Many took advantage of the offer. Upon their purchase, they were pleasantly surprised to be awarded with a $2-off certificate at the Minit Lube next door. How fortuitous. When they got their bill after the oil change, they presented their $2-off certificate.

The quick-lube place got several dozen redemptions. But the ROMI was negative. The way this promotion was executed, it ended up only discounting people who were going to pay full price anyway. No new customers resulted from this promotion. If you have a new business and not a great deal of awareness in

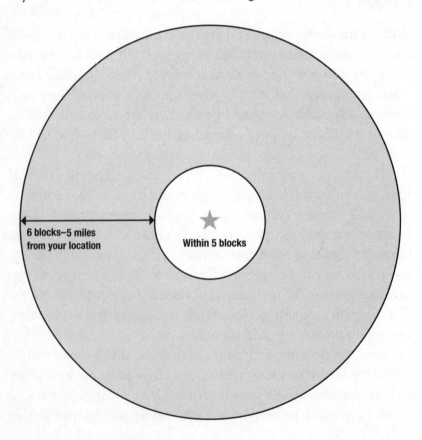

your community, cross-promoting in your backyard may make sense. For a more mature store or business, you want to think of a donut shape. Place your store in the middle of the donut hole, which you can think of as a two- to five-block radius. Stores in that circle are too close. Then you have the donut from beyond the hole to about three or four miles out. That's where you should place your efforts from a geographical point of view.

Credibility

One of the biggest advantages of a cross-promotion is that it allows you to protect your price credibility. One of the biggest problems facing businesses today is discounting, because your customers become addicted to the discount and then refuse to pay full price ever again. With a cross-promotion, on the other hand, you can offer a special savings of some kind, but because the cross-promotion partner is handing out your offer, he takes full credit for the special offer. You've *transferred the responsibility of the discount* to the other merchant, and your regular-price credibility is protected.

Setting Up the Promotion

How do you get other merchants to hand out your advertising for you for free? You have to approach them properly. Here's an example of what I might use:

> My name is Jeff Slutsky with Jeff's Flower Shop down the street. I saw a program that worked for someone else, and I wanted to run it by you. (Show a sample of the other promotion.) I would like to offer you the opportunity to provide your customers something extra—a way to give them a little bit more for their money and a great way for you to personally thank them for being your customers. What do you think?

At this point, you wait for the person to come back with something like "Well, it sounds great, but how much is this going to cost?" This response usually happens about ninety-nine out of one hundred times. So you respond, "Well, let me ask you this: If it were *free*, would you do it?" Then the'll say something like "Free? Sure, why not?" You then simply respond with "Fair enough," and the promotion is a done deal. Before you leave, get his weekly customer count, so that you know how many pieces have to be printed. Also, be sure to get a couple of copies of the business logo. That way you can print it right on the certificate. Other useful information to get is the correct spelling of the business manager or owner's name or even a signature to put on the piece. Then you can make the top of the certificate read: "This Special Thank You Is Compliments of [Logo] and [Signature], Owner [or Manager]." By putting both the merchant's name and the owner's or manager's name on the certificate, you transfer responsibility twice, and that person has a very personal reason for making sure all of the pieces get distributed to his customers.

To get a little practice in, I suggest setting up your first few promotions with some good friends. They don't have to be high-priority cross-promotion partners, because the purpose of these promotions is to give you practice setting them up and getting the materials printed and delivered.

The Reverse Cross-promotion

A jewelry store located in a mall in Indiana competed with more than a dozen others in its marketplace. The challenge for the owner was to add some kind of cost-effective value to motivate shoppers to commit to his engagement rings instead of looking at all the other stores. The Street Fighter Solution was the "wedding package."

The manager went to his friends who also served the wedding market. He asked them what it would be worth to them to have access to people in the market for wedding services at the point when they first decided to get married. Of course, it was a loaded question. The first step on the marriage-go-round is the engagement ring. This manager had access to a group of customers that other businesses find very valuable. But instead of asking these businesses to buy advertising to reach this group, he wanted an exclusive offer from their businesses. He asked for something of significant value to the couple (either a discount or value added), but which also made sense to the vendors if they got advance access to potential wedding business.

The jewelry store manager created a packet of offers. The envelope and inserts had the same look and feel as a nice wedding invitation. Inside were a dozen pieces that provided exclusive offers from the bakery, the bridal shop, the tux shop, the photographer, the limousine service, the banquet hall, the travel agency, the florist, the invitation printer, the dance studio, and the weight loss center. The pieces were printed for free by the invitation printer, who received placement on the top of the packet for the additional contribution.

The value of this package was over $1,000, including some discounts and some freebies. Now when a happy couple was first looking for an engagement ring but wanted to continue looking because the ring cost several hundred dollars more than they wanted to spend, he had a sweetener: "If you go with this ring today, we have this special wedding packet that is worth over $1,000 in savings on your wedding." It made a great closing tool for the manager, and the cost to the jewelry store was nothing. This promotion had a much higher perceived value than a $200 discount and was much more profitable.

Nonmerchants

It's not just retailers that can use these types of ideas. With a little massaging and tweaking, you can make them work in a variety of situations. Consider Edye, a drug representative for a major pharmaceutical company. Her job depends on getting access to busy doctors so that she can make a five-minute presentation (called detailing) about a specific medication. There was a time when the company provided spiffs and freebies to help reps gain access to the doctors, but times have changed, and such incentives have been taken from the budget.

Edye knew that about half of her four hundred doctors played golf. With no budget to buy golf items, her Street Fighter Solution was to approach a retail chain of golf equipment stores in town. She asked the regional manager how valuable it would be to get several hundred doctors to visit one of its area stores. The regional manager knew that a doctor represented a couple thousand dollars in sales over an eighteen-month period. (He obviously did the exercise to determine the value of a new customer.)

Edye suggested that he give her two hundred certificates good for a box of free Titleist golf balls. Each box had a retail

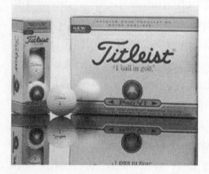

value, then, of about $25. The golf store's cost was around $10 per box. Edye gave the gift certificates (which had an expiration date of only two weeks) to her doctors; many of them actually drove across town to redeem their certificates. In order for the certificate to be valid, Edye had to present to the doctor in person, and it had to be signed by the doctor. She was able to get face-to-face with more doctors, and the golf store chain got many new customers for very little money.

She also used the same idea to gain favor with the receptionists and nurses in the doctors' offices. These people are the gatekeepers, and the better her relationship with them, the more effectively she can do her job. A manicurist was just starting out at a local hair salon and had more time than money to promote her new venture. Edye suggested that she give her one hundred certificates for

> Give it away free, and they will come.

free manicures. Many of the nurses who would redeem these might end up being repeat customers. Plus, even though the manicure would be free, the manicurist would still get some tips. Edye was able to get a couple thousand dollars' worth of free manicures, which made her very popular among the staff. And the fledgling manicurist got her business off the ground in less than a month.

Applications Beyond

You can apply this tactic to nonretailers such as insurance agencies, real-estate agencies, remodeling businesses, and more. Think about your end users and why they would be in the market for your services? What life-changing event would cause someone to actually seek out an insurance agent or financial planner? In my case, it was the birth of my triplets: C.J., Natalie, and Eli. With a

total of five children, life got a little more complicated. Both my wife and I needed to dramatically increase our life insurance and medical insurance. I opened three additional 529 college fund accounts. We remodeled a few rooms in the house and then finished off the basement to add more livable room. And, of course, we traded in my sports car for a minivan.

If you're selling any of those services, how could you reach someone like me at this point in my life? Anyone who has a new baby has new needs. The same applies with other life-changing events, including pregnancy, graduation from high school or college, marriage, divorce, retirement (or nearing retirement), and death. Now fast-forward twenty-two months and add another daughter. The process starts all over again.

What cross-promotion partners would you want to pursue? Think in terms of what businesses or organizations would people seek when going through a given life change. What kind of value added could you provide to make it worth these businesses' efforts to refer you to their customers? What is the potential ROMI from such an effort done right?

Seasonal Promotions

Not all businesses see their customers equally throughout the year. For example, to get the most exposure from cross-promoting with a card shop, florist, jewelry store, candy store, and photo finishing store, you might want to consider setting up your promotions before Valentine's Day, Easter, Mother's Day, and Christmas. (You may want to add Sweetest Day.) If you want more exposure toward the beginning of the year, cross-promote with businesses that are associated with New Year's resolutions, including health clubs, weight loss businesses, and smoking cessation clinics. In early April, you'll get a lot of action from lawn and garden services, mulch suppliers, tanning salons, and tax return preparers. If you need to pick up business in late October, you should cross-promote with a costume shop. They have one big season during the year, and it's the week before Halloween.

The difference in your ROMI from doing a cross-promotion any time or doing a cross-promotion at the right time for a given type of partner can be ten to twenty times more. Think three months ahead in your planning so that you can identify with whom and when you want to promote to maximize your efforts and your return on your marketing investment.

In-the-loop Promotion

Sometimes you get more by helping your competitor. That may sound strange, but there are special situations where promoting your competitor will help increase your sales. One example of this is the "in-the-loop" promotion. The first time I used this type of promotion was when I was part owner of a nightclub. Most of our customers, even the regulars, did a certain amount of barhopping. We knew the club was one of perhaps twenty that they could visit in a given night.

The idea behind "in the loop" was to create an association of nightclub owners with whom we had a good relationship. There were six of us in all. We had a special certificate created that was given to our customers when they left our club. The other five establishments would do the same. The offer on the promotional piece was good at any of the other five operations for that night. This offer would provide an incentive for those customers leaving to go elsewhere to choose one of the night-clubs in the loop. So, as customers around town started to bar-hop, once they hopped into the establishment of one of our six participants, our group would capture that customer and keep them in our loop.

Each club owner could track the results, because the customer would redeem the certificate. Since there were incentives to keep a customer in the loop of the six participating clubs, the market share of the six increased, as did their sales.

A more recent example of this in-the-loop promotion came up when a regional fast-food hamburger restaurant, the top franchisee in the chain, found out that a new competitor was moving into the market. This regional fast-food hamburger restaurant was also in competition with a national hamburger franchise down the street. The national hamburger franchise, like the regional competitor, was on the short list of the highest-volume units in its chain.

Since both hamburger restaurants were going to face competition from a new player, they began to question how they could work together. Here are a few of the suggestions we gave to them:

1. Promote your old competitor. During the grand opening week of the new competitor, the two handed out certificates to their customers promoting the other's restaurant. The purpose was to keep people from trying the new place.
2. Shut down for one lunch day-part (shift). That's right, shut down. Then put up a banner that says "In honor of our new neighbor, we're closed. Go visit them." With both high-volume places shut down, the only place open will be the new place. And since it's likely that it wasn't expecting to have 100 percent of the market share that lunch, customers will probably wait a very long time for their food. They will get annoyed at the slow service. They'll get angry. And since their first experience with this new competitor is likely to be negative, they may vow never to return.

Exercise

Step One

On a piece of paper, write down the names of twenty-five businesses that you feel would make a good cross-promotion partner for you in your area. These are businesses only; nonprofit groups, schools, and associations will be used for different types of promotions in a later chapter.

Step Two

Place a check mark in front of any of the businesses on your list if its manager, owner, or someone of major influence is one of your regular customers or is a personal friend, relative, or acquaintance. You don't have to be best of friends, but count someone as a friend if you would acknowledge that person if you saw each other out somewhere.

Action Plan

1. Conduct a business card drawing for four weeks. This is your first step.
   a. Do it now. I'll wait.
2. Start setting up cross-promotions once every seven to ten days.
   a. Not all promotions will be merchant certificates (see other chapters).
   b. Start with the businesses that you gave checkmarks in the exercise above.
   c. Then go with the business cards from your drawing.
3. Track the response of each promotion. Determine how many new customers each promotion generated and the amount of new sales generated.
4. Use a bounce-back certificate to identify repeat buyers and distinguish them from new customers.

6

DIRECT MAIL THAT WON'T GET TRASHED

Effective direct mail allows you to target both existing and potential new customers using a printed piece or even a three-dimensional item. With the right list of prospects, you can implement a Street Fighter Marketing one-on-one campaign geared to individual buying habits and preferences. You can focus your effort both demographically and geographically with little waste. Unlike mass media, you can reach as few or as many potential buyers as you want, since you choose the audience size.

The big problem with direct mail is that the vast majority of it ends up in the garbage. The reason why is that most direct mail looks like junk mail. To get your message read and acted upon, your mailing pieces must be compelling. An effective mailing piece comprises a strong benefit headline, relevant body copy, an eye-catching graphic, and a powerful call to action. If one of these four elements falls short, your piece falls into the trash bin.

POSTCARD PROCREATION

Most mailing pieces get tossed even before the envelope is opened. For that reason, a well-done postcard offers you some advantages over a flyer or a letter in an envelope. A postcard gives you the opportunity to expose your message to the reader without him having to open an envelope. If you have a compelling graphic and headline, you have a decent chance of the reader taking a little time with your piece. The other big advantage is cost. A postcard costs very little to produce, even in full color. Plus, a standard-size postcard costs only 26¢ to mail first class. You can design and order postcards entirely over the web without having to leave your business. They make a great way to stay in touch with a list of customers or prospects on a regular basis, and are very good at helping you supplement other types of contact.

Another critical advantage for postcards is speed. You can design, print, address, and mail your postcards in a very short period of time, which allows you to take advantage of unique opportunities. But more important, since it takes very little effort to have an effective postcard mailing program, you're more likely to do it regularly.

One of our all-time favorite postcard mailings was done by the owner of a quick-print store in Ohio. While she was in Las Vegas for her annual quick-printer's convention, she bought a case of picture postcards from the MGM Grand. She brought them back to her shop and had her kids hand address them with the names of four hundred businesses that were *not* her customers. The message on the back of the postcard read, "Don't gamble with your printing needs. Bring in this postcard for a 10 percent savings on your first printing order." She received one hundred redemptions! That's a 25 percent return. The reason? It didn't look like junk mail. If you got a picture postcard from

Vegas, you'd probably ask yourself, "Who do I know in Vegas, and how much did they win?" You would then turn it over to see who it was from and see the headline: "Don't gamble with your [insert the name of your service]." You'd remember the offer. Because the offer required redemption of the postcard, as if it were a coupon, she knew exactly what her return on her investment was for this promotion.

While I was in Nashville addressing a group of real-estate agents from all over the United States, I told them the Las Vegas postcard story. Then I gave them an assignment to find picture postcards at the venue, make up a list of twenty-five potential clients, create a headline that tied into the picture on the postcard, and mail the postcards from Nashville. One creative group found postcards with horses running through a pasture. Their headline was "Don't horse around when you want to sell your home fast."

A real-estate agent mailed a simple postcard to several hundred homes. He was offering a free home warranty for listing with him. But the postcard was boring. It was black ink on gray card stock and didn't look particularly appealing. As expected, 100 percent of his mailing was trashed. A week later, those same homes received an envelope from the same guy. Inside the envelope was the same postcard, only it had been crumpled up and then flattened. Attached to the crumpled postcard was a yellow sticky note that read "Please don't throw this out again! This is important." People must have been saying to themselves, "Is this guy going through the trash? He must really know the neighborhood. We gotta give him a call!"

Another clever use of an inexpensive postcard mailing was done by a scuba store in San Francisco that had planned a diving trip to Maui. Many customers inquired about the trip, but only a third, as expected, actually signed up for it. The store owner took the list of people who couldn't make it that time. From Maui, he mailed picture postcards showing the reef and wrote a brief message about what a wonderful time they were having. What a great way to build up strong interest for future trips. Also, while there, he gave each of his participants three post- cards with postage and asked them to write a wish-you-were- here message to their scuba friends back home. It was a great way to generate referral business.

A colleague of ours, Somers White, would send us postcards from places like China and France. The idea impressed us so much that we used it when we were on a speaking tour in Singa- pore and Malaysia. I took preprinted address labels of twenty- five prospects that were on the fence about booking me as their keynote speaker. From Singapore, I mailed twenty-five picture postcards with a brief message about how well the speaking tour was going. I actually returned home before the postcards were delivered to the prospects, but when my sales force followed up by phone, every one of them remembered my postcard from Sin- gapore. The return on investment in this case was that it allowed the salespeople to more easily connect with the prospects.

When we first started doing postcard mailings to our data- base list, the response was weak. In retrospect, the reason was that the postcard content just didn't have enough benefit or piz- zazz to do any good. We would order five thousand postcards at a time to get a good price. But our main lists totaled no more than one thousand. This meant that the front side of the post- card was the same for multiple mailings. We printed the reverse side with a different message each time. And because we had to order such a large quantity, we kept the full-color front very generic, so that it would have some shelf life. One version was a picture of three of our books. On paper, the costs looked good in producing the pieces. But the ROMI turned out to be weak, so the low cost was irrelevant.

Then we were referred to a new printing supplier online, VistaPrint, which allowed us to buy as few as one hundred full-color postcards at the same unit price as the five thousand we ordered before (when on sale). Plus, with these quantities, it would print the back side in black and white for no charge (a full-color back would basically double the price). Consequently, we could tailor the message each time, both front and back.

VistaPrint has a web-based development and production capability. Once on its site, you use its online software to create several different types of marketing items, including standard or oversize postcards, presentation folders, business cards, note cards, refrigerator magnets, and return address labels. The website provides templates that make it very easy to create these items using its artwork, including over seventy thousand royalty-free photos and illustrations, or by uploading your own.

One of its key marketing tactics is to offer 250 free business cards to anybody at anytime. This is an ongoing special.

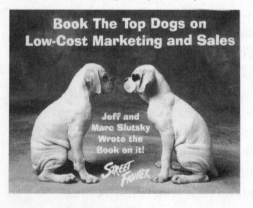

It gets people to its site, and, as a result, visitors learn about the company's other available items. Plus, VistaPrint usually offers several other free items to get people to try them out, like one hundred free standard-size postcards. To create an account and get some free samples, go to our website: www.streetfightermarketing.com. In the banner, you'll see a direct link to the VistaPrint website. This will allow you to get several free items to try them out. (Of course, we'll get credit for anything you order.)

With the VistaPrint program, you can order as few as one hundred standard-size postcards (which require 26¢ to mail) or fifty oversize postcards. With this affordable quantity, you can create targeted campaigns to small groups of your database. Here's the interesting thing: Once you place your first order, you get the company's catalog and notice of its email specials. VistaPrint is constantly running specials to get you to buy its other items. We would order these items, and, after paying a small onetime charge to use an uploaded graphic for the first time, we could use that graphic again at no extra cost.

Once, the company promoted a special to us, and we were able to order the following items: 100 standard-size post-cards, 50 oversize postcards, 25 business card size magnets, 10 large magnets, 10 note cards, 10 folded note cards, 10 invitations, and 1 rubber stamp. Total cost: $0. Shipping and handling for slow delivery: $10.45. That's a lot of marketing stuff for under $11.00. Then we were able to log on four days in a row and reorder at the same price. The bottom line here is that we were able to order a total of 500 standard and 250 oversize postcards in addition to all the other items for about $55. And even when we needed greater quantities, once they were on sale, 500 postcards cost only $48.

The one other advantage of using this website is that it really helps to stir your creativity. Sending our generic postcard probably didn't generate all that much attention. But the site has templates for a variety of different industries. The postcard that worked the best for us was made for pet care. We then used a "top dog" take in the headline. This postcard got a number of inbound calls, several of which led to eventual sales. Well, if two dogs worked, how about a graphic with five dogs? Or one with one big wrinkly dog and a kitten and a jet? The jet postcard is sent to clients who already know us, because we have a signature story about having to lease a private jet to make a gig.

Another experiment that we did with other graphics was having the back side of the postcard printed in gray scale, which

Figure 2 Standard-size postcard with full color on front and gray scale on the back, with basic design and graphics from a generic template.

is free (for full color on the back, it cost another $10). We had postcards printed both ways and found no increase in response with the color versus the gray.

With full-color postcards printed in quantities as low as fifty, you have other opportunities for specialized mailings. For

example, Eddy Rajczyk runs Curb Light Appeal, a company that provides landscape lighting. Once he does a job in a given neighborhood, he puts up a yard sign for about a month, which gets the attention of all the neighbors. To speed the neighborhood awareness along, Eddy mails out postcards to twenty-five to fifty homes in the neighborhood. The photo on the front is of the neighboring home at dusk, showing off all the new landscape lighting. Another shot appears on the back in black and white with body copy that tells them that their neighbor (actual name and address) has just installed landscape lighting. It also provides the suggestion, "Take a look for yourself and give us a call, so we can give you ideas on how to dramatically enhance the beauty of your home, too." Of course, this is done with permission of the customer, but the price Eddy quotes reflects the customer's willingness to help promote the company. In nearly every case, the customer is thrilled to share his newly lit landscape with the neighborhood.

The Curb Light Appeal mailing has a very short run but is highly targeted geographically. It follows actual work and is accompanied by the placement of a yard sign that reinforces the message. It's very inexpensive, but it provides one of the highest ROMIs you can get because of the unique nature of the mailing. This approach can work for just about any home repair or improvement, including landscaping, window replacements, pool or spa installations, room additions, new furniture, basement remodeling, and so on. It can also work for any home improvement that enhances the overall value of the home, like replacing the furnace with a more energy efficient one or installing a fireplace insert, new carpeting, and drapes. You could also do this with door hangers if you have the time to personally deliver the pieces.

Expand the concept even more. A car dealer sells a brand-new luxury car to someone. The neighbors are envious for about a week or two. With permission, the dealer gets addresses of a couple dozen neighbors and sends out a custom postcard. It has a picture of their neighbor standing in front of his or her new car. It's a great way to proactively speed along the referral process. If any neighbor calls this salesperson about a car and buys, the original customer gets a reward of some kind. The point is that you don't wait for the happy customer to tell his neighbors and friends. You work that relationship at the point your customer is most excited about the purchase and most likely to work with you in creating this mini-mailing campaign.

The same approach can be done in a business-to-business setting. After twenty-five years of furnishing our office with hand-me-downs, used items, and military surplus, we decided to upscale. Corporate Interior Concepts provided us brand-new furniture: desks, workstations, file cabinets, chairs, and so forth. The entire office was redone, and it looks super. Any vendor or colleague who had been to our office knew how postapocalyptic it had looked. So we sent a postcard showing the before and after to a list of vendors and colleagues. In this case, we suggested that CIC's salespeople follow up each of those postcards with a phone call, and when CIC did that, they set up appointments to visit prospective customers in person and assess their needs. There's something very special about seeing yourself and your office with your new surroundings on a full-color postcard.

GET THE ENVELOPE OPENED

There's also a hybrid direct mail that you initiate on the internet but which results in a printed piece actually being delivered by the postal service. Consider our client who each year used to mail out about three hundred expensive presentation folders that explained the special service it provided. Though the mailing yielded results when combined with follow-up phone calls, each piece cost about $10 delivered. Even at that, some of the three hundred targets never opened the envelope. To improve the ROMI on this effort, we suggested that our client use just the cover letter delivered via certified mail by the U.S. Postal Service.

The first certified mailing was a printed letter in a standard #10 business envelope using the green-bordered certified-mailing stickers. The postage, including the certification fee, was $2.79 each plus printing. For the total price, add the cost of folding, stuffing, and standing in line at the post office. Though an expensive piece for a single letter, the results were dramatic. Nearly every piece was opened. The inbound calls nearly doubled, which obviously saved a lot of time in the follow-up.

The real breakthrough came when we suggested that our client do the entire mailing process online at www.usps.com. That would mean no stuffing, no stamping, no printing, no folding, and, most important, no going to the local post office and standing in line. It cost a little more per piece to do it this way, but the savings in time was well worth it. The mailing piece itself was printed by the postal service on certified mail paper stock, which made the letter look even more official. The mailing list was uploaded from the client's database. The certified letter looks like official government business. It's delivered by the letter carrier, requires a signature, and beckons to be opened. The bottom line: The overall response was about 20 percent better than the more expensive folder mailing, and the client had an overall savings of $2,265, or about 75 percent. The strategy was a winner because it provided better results, saved time, and cost less money.

The certified letter is obviously an expensive mailing piece compared to a standard first-class envelope and even compared to mailing a presentation folder. But when you evaluate it based on the return, the additional cost was more than justified. So although many Street Fighter Solutions are intended to find a cheaper marketing tactic, you still may find that paying more provides you a greater return on your marketing investment.

INVITATIONS

One piece of mail that seems to always get opened and read is an invitation—in particular, a wedding invitation. Why is that? After all, a wedding invitation is really like any other form of solicitation. It's an ad. Your call to action is usually for the invitee to send in a response. But whether the invitee attends or not, he is obliged to send a gift. Yet people seem to get very excited when they receive a wedding invitation.

So if you want your message to get read, make it look like a wedding invitation. It doesn't have to be like the oversize, oddly shaped, parchment-and-ribbons invitation, either. A simple one like those that you can find on vistaprint.com or other wedding invitation websites will do just fine. (Sometimes you can get a discontinued line for a fraction of the original cost.)

Hand address your invitations. If you can do calligraphy, that would be great, but it is not necessary. Just don't use a computer label, though. *The return address on the back flap should be that flowery cursive typeface (like this)*. Also, don't include your business name, just your street address. And don't use a meter for postage. Use a "Love" stamp. These steps will get your invitation opened. And when it is, the invitee will see that it's an "invitation" to discover your value or some kind of tie-in like that.

GREETING CARDS

Like invitations, another type of mail piece that usually gets opened is greeting cards. The advantages are: They're relatively cheap, they're readily available at any card shop and many other stores, they're high-quality printed pieces, they're available in a great variety, and they almost always get opened and read. Of course, the best time to buy a specific greeting card is when it's out of season. Just save them for the following year. In order to make an impact, you want to use these greeting cards in unusual ways.

Scott Friedman, a professional speaker based in Golden, Colorado, told us, "I send out Thanksgiving cards in November instead of Christmas and Hanukkah cards in December. All my clients get tons of cards in late December, but they usually get only one Thanksgiving card a month earlier. And they remember my card more than all of the others."

A local hair stylist used greeting cards when he switched salons. Changing from the northern part of the city to a new salon just south of downtown, he was disappointed that eighteen special customers didn't make the switch. Each month he would send a different greeting card and simply write the message "I miss you." One month he mailed only his business card with that same message on the back. Over the following twelve months, all eighteen returned to his styling chair.

Valentine's Day is an opportunity to share your feelings with your customers and clients. The card should be on the lighter side. Be sure to write a business response on the inside of the card, such as, "We love doing business with you," or "For a sweetheart of a deal, give me a call . . ." It's best to have the card signed by several key people in your organization or sign it as your business. You don't want to give anyone the wrong impression!

Another idea is to have a small inventory of special greeting cards that you can use as the need arises. These would include: condolences, get well soon, congratulations, happy birthday, and happy anniversary (which can be used for wedding anniversaries or the anniversary of employment). Warning: If you're planning to use a wedding anniversary card for a client you haven't been in touch with for a while, it's a good idea to make sure that person is still married. It could be really embarrassing if you sent an anniversary card when you should have sent a condolence card. When our weekly column was first published, several of our vendors clipped it, put it in a congratulations card, and mailed it to us. It certainly was noticed!

Just when we finally got used to Sweetest Day, they came out with Boss's Day. Well, fortunately, we don't have to worry about that one. But it does create an opportunity. Think of the impact you would make sending a Boss's Day card to some of your key customers or clients with the message "You're the boss."

It seems that just about every business sends out Christmas cards, and it's very likely that not one makes any kind of impact with the customer. The reason is simple: There are too many of them. Your card is mixed up with dozens, if not hundreds, of others. But what if there was one Christmas card that actually generated a bunch of business? Howard Eichenwald, a computer consultant based in Overland Park, Kansas, told us about a Christmas card that one of his uncles received. Apparently, the company mailed five hundred cards, prepared in advance, every year. Early in October, the envelopes were all hand addressed and stamped with a Christmas stamp. Then they were stored it the back room until early December, when they were mailed.

One year the company prepared the Christmas cards as always. However, it forgot to mail them. The following May, someone was looking for something in the back room and came across the five hundred Christmas cards. After discussing it for a moment, the staff decided that instead of throwing them in the trash, they would throw them in the mail. Within a week, most of the company's five hundred customers started getting their Christmas cards. May is generally the company's slow time, but suddenly it was inundated with phone calls. Most of its customers blamed the card's late arrival on the postal service. Totally unfair in this case, but no one bothered to set them straight. Nearly everyone who got a card called to say, "You won't believe what the post office did to your Christmas card this year."

Not wanting to let a unique opportunity go to waste, the salespeople would ask if they needed anything and recommend some of the company's specials. What usually was its worst time of the year became one of its most profitable times of the year. And it was all due to a mistake.

3D

A totally different way of getting your mailer noticed is to go with something that has some bulk to it. Of course, this will cost you more both for the mailing item and the postage, so you'll want to be selective where you send it. Our first exposure to the power of this approach came years ago when our very first book, *Streetfighting: Low-cost Advertising/Promotion Strategies for Your Business,* went out of print. Compared to several of our newer books, this one was out of date. Yet it still had some great information. And we had a basement full of them. So we decided to mail out autographed copies to a list of businesses that we wanted to do business with.

We started out sending five a day, along with a cover letter and a few pieces of promotional material. The goal was to mail out three hundred. A book is less likely to get tossed out than junk mail, and we started getting calls. First, Arby's called and ordered three hundred copies. That alone showed us a nice ROMI on the mailing effort. Arby's is still a client to this day. Plus, we picked up several speeches and some consulting work.

When doing this type of more expensive mailing, you obviously want to test the waters before you send out a lot. After the first fifty books, we knew we had a winner, so we continued the program.

What useful items do you have in your organization that potential customers would find a real use for? Free samples are always a great way of getting people's attention.

THE LIST

Your mailing list is as important to a successful direct mailing as the mailing piece itself. The cleaner the list is, the less it will cost you every time you mail. For that reason, it's a good idea to mail first class on a regular basis, so you'll get the returned pieces that were not deliverable. This allows you to either delete that contact from your database or update the contact's information with a current deliverable address. The ability to update information is particularly important when you rent a list. No matter how current that list may be, you'll probably see a fair amount of outdated addresses on it.

You'll get a much greater return when you have a specific contact in the address instead of just a title or "occupant." How much more effective depends on a number of factors, so it's a good idea to do a split test and compare results. If you have 500 names, mail 250 to the "occupant" or "marketing director" or any generic contact. Address the other 250 to the actual contact, which means that you'll have to spend the extra money for those names. Make sure that you have a strong call to action in your mail piece and see which half provides a better response. Assuming that the list with the names pulls better, you will want to determine how much better. What was the increased return on your investment versus the generic version? After you subtract the additional cost of the list with the actual contacts, you can see which gave you the best return.

If you plan a more costly type of mailing where the mailer and the postage will cost you a significant amount of money (like our book mailing), you should do a first-class postcard mailing to that list first. Before you spend $5 or more on a mailer, it just makes sense to spend the 26¢ in postage for a postcard to clean the list. Your postcard can even be used to make the recipient aware that in a week he'll receive this valuable item in the mail. In that way, your postcard list tester also does double duty in making your more expensive mailer a little more effective.

Another interesting test would be to see how different-size postcards compare with each other. Split your list between the standard-size post card, which mails for 26¢, and the oversize postcard, which mails for 41¢. The cost of the oversize postcard is a little more as well. However, the oversize postcard is more than twice the size and will be a lot more visible in a pile of mail when received. Use the same graphics and expand the copy into the extra space, as long as the copy provides benefits to the reader. Again, use a strong call to action for both mailings to get accurate results regarding the importance of the postcard size.

Another element that you can test is the effect of the frequency of mailing. Direct mail often works best when the recipient receives a number of pieces over time. A potential customer may need to see your message repeatedly before he decides to respond. It also may be that on the sixth mailing, your prospect is now in the market for your service, so your mailing piece has more relevance at that point. You want to mix up your mailers, so that the customer doesn't become immune to them. But at the same time, you want some consistency, so that in some way the piece is identifiable with your business. You could use the same logo, slogan, colors, or other branding elements.

MARRIAGE MAILERS

There are several group mailing programs available that allow you to be one of many pieces in the envelope. The cost is generally reasonable, and because you are part of a number of offerings, you might get some exposure that you might not see with a solo mailer.

Most of these pieces usually are in the form of some kind of coupon. This is good, in that it allows you to track the results via the coupon's redemption. The downside of sending out coupons is that if you constantly offer coupons via mass advertising and mass mail, you'll begin to condition your customers to always wait for the deal. Too much couponing will destroy your price credibility.

There are also specialty direct-mail pieces for specific occasions. There are several services available that target new moves by zip code. This method can be very effective for many types of local businesses, in that it allows them to get first contact with a brand-new potential customer. In this case, a real strong introductory offer won't hurt your company's price credibility, because getting the attention of someone new to the neighborhood is a believable reason to offer a onetime discount. Again, you must track your results and evaluate this promotion's ROMI based on the cost against how much new business it brought in to your company.

A similar service is usually available for special events such as weddings. If you service that industry, a marriage mailer with many offerings from a variety of wedding-oriented businesses will attract the attention of a bride-to-be. Photographers, entertainment, reception halls, bridal shops, tux shops, limo services, videographers, travel agencies, party rentals, caterers, invitation printers, dance instructors, and so on are all trying to reach the same people. Ideally, you want to use a mailing service that will offer your business exclusivity for its service.

If you want to do your own mailing, you might team up with some of the better businesses near you that offer services that can be associated with yours, as demonstrated by those businesses mentioned above. Teaming up will allow you to share the cost of a more elaborate mailer.

REFERRAL MAILINGS

This approach is used by two noncompeting businesses that have a good relationship with each other. They each do a mailing for the other to introduce the other to their customers. For example, Shep Hyken, the author of *Moments of Magic*, is a wonderful speaker on customer service. We don't offer the information that Shep does, but most of our clients have a need for it. And most of his customers could use a program on low-cost marketing or sales training. We each provided the other a list of fifty clients that we felt would have a strong interest in each other's area of expertise. After a few changes to the list, Shep provided us fifty autographed copies of his book, and we did the same for him. We then mailed his book to our clients with a cover letter suggesting that Shep would be a great speaker at their next event. He did the same for us.

After the mailing, the respective sales forces would follow up by phone. Though a more expensive mailing, it provides a high ROMI because you are referred to potential customers by a business they already know and trust. Every few months, we continued to do this type of program with several other speaker buddies of ours. Our clients loved it because they kept getting free auto-graphed books. It worked so well that we did the same mailing idea with T. Scott Gross, author of *Outrageous Service,* as well as with Bob Losyk, author of *Managing a Changing Workforce.*

GETTING SOMEONE TO MAIL ON YOUR BEHALF

While working with Consumers' Choice Award of Indianapo-lis, we were able to develop a good relationship with the Greater Indianapolis Chamber of Commerce. The first year the award was introduced to Indy was toughest, because it had no credibility. We had our client join the chamber as a gold member and then went to meet the VP of marketing in person to let him know what we were doing. We had a list of roughly three hundred local busi-nesses that won the award, according to an independent survey commissioned by the company. These were the top two or three businesses in each business category. We also knew that only 12 percent of that group were members of the chamber.

We asked the chamber to mail a letter of congratulations to each of the three hundred winners. We also offered a member-to-member discount on the program's licensing fee. The savings would be close to the cost of the membership dues for joining the chamber. Though the discounts cost Consumers' Choice Award, more of its winners became licensees, and the chamber's letter lent an increased degree awareness of and credibility to the pro-gram. The following year, Consumer's Choice Award did the same thing, and there was a notable increase in interest from the group immediately following the chamber's letter.

As an exercise, determine at least ten local businesses or organizations whose membership or customer base provide an ideal source of new customers for your business. Think of what you have to offer that business or group. It could be exposure to your customer base via direct mail or other means, or perhaps free samples of your product or service to provide as an added value to their customers. In return, you want those groups to do a targeted mailing on your behalf, introducing your business. It won't be perceived as junk mail, because the recipient will recognize the business that is sending the piece.

NEW NEIGHBORS PROGRAM

Regardless of how good a business is and how well it serves customers, it is going to lose up to 25 percent of its customer base each year. Add in losses due to aggressive competition, and your total "customer inventory" could be shrinking by as much as 50 percent annually. Jay Siff, president of Moving Targets, a direct-mail advertising company based in Perkasie, Pennsylvania, points to the crucial need to recruit fresh replacements for a disappearing customer base. What is Siff's secret weapon? New residents! He says that new residents should be your prime sales prospects. During their first six months in a new home, they spend up to ten times more on a wide range of products and services than established residents spend in two years. New residents are easily identifiable, fully reachable, ready to embrace change, free of old buying habits, and very susceptible to warm-hearted welcome messages.

Siff makes the following suggestions about tapping this rich resource: First, targeted direct mail works. A persuasive direct mail campaign that puts a friendly, caring face on your business will attract new residents to your stores. Next, present a generous offer with a human touch. The more restriction free an offer is, the better it works. A personal touch and credibility are almost always necessary for high response. Also, small numbers yield significant sales. A customized offer mailed to an updated and accurate list of new residents' names and addresses is essential. A relatively small number of these ready-to-spend newcomers are required to produce significant sales. It's worth your effort because new-residents-turned-customers are worth a great deal more than other consumers. The current cost of premier welcome-neighbor mailing packages ranges from $1 to $2 per unit. As many as 25 percent will act positively on the offer.

On average, these new neighbors are loyal—sticking with their first picks longer than new customers acquired from other sources. Over the long term, they are five times more likely to become regular customers. Newly arrived families have powerful needs to replace favorite places to shop, eat, bank, work out, get their hair cut, have fun, get the car serviced, or the dog groomed. These modern nomads are motivated to make new friends, build new loyalties, and establish new buying habits—to do everything possible to feel as though they belong in their new surroundings. The bottom line is that, when you are looking for new customers, they're the best of the best!

To support the local direct mail effort corporations can use the Agilis Marketing Suite from Saepio Technologies that was mentioned in the previous chapter for print advertising [www .saepio.com (877) 468-7613 toll free]. The direct mail function with this online solution not only allows you to create templates that your local business units can customize for their local marketplace, but Saepio can set up this function so that your local unit operators can merge it with a mailing list, print, post, and mail . . . all with just a few clicks of the mouse. If a mailing list is needed, they tie the function into purchasing a list that meets the demographic criteria that you set up. The local operator can buy all these functions with a credit card, purchase order, or permission code depending on your operation. For supporting all aspects of local marketing from the corporate level, for businesses of more than fifty units, you really need to check these guys out. You can request a demo on their website.

7

INSIDER MARKETING

Some of the best Street Fighter Marketing Solutions can be done on-site. The obvious advantage to these types of promotions is that you have total control over their implementation, since you are not promoting in conjunction with another merchant or organization. Plus, anytime you can arrange a low-cost promotion that does not require you to leave your operation to do it, you've met one critical condition of a Street Fighter Solution with local marketing: Your investment of time is minimal.

EMPLOYEE CONTEST SOLUTIONS

The employee incentive contest is a fail-safe idea that can be done several times a year. It takes very little time to set up and almost always provides a super return. First, create certificates that have a strong offer on your product or service. This offer should be better than any standard coupon or discount that you would use. The actual printed piece can be one-fourth of a piece of paper and works best when printed on colored card stock with one color of ink. This special certificate contains a line at the bottom for your employees' signatures and a date.

Participation in the contest is totally voluntary. Any full- or part-time employee can participate. You start by giving each participating employee fifty certificates. They sign them. Then you explain that they can hand them out on their own time and beyond the perimeter of your parking lot. Tell them to give the certificates to friends, family, and anybody else they come in contact with: the postman, the cashier, and so on. Their signature authorizes the special discount.

Now You Have a Friend At

(Insert your logo)

As a friend of our valued employee,

You are entitled to:

(Insert the offer)

This offer is good only at (insert name and address of business). Only one certificate per person per visit. Cannot be combined with any other special or discount. Offer expires in 30 days.

Authorized by _____ Date _____
Our Valued Employee

The contest can run for four weeks. If a given employee runs out of cards, you give him or her more. The results of the contest are based on redemptions. The employee with the most redemptions that week wins the first-place prize, the employee with the second most redemptions gets the second-place prize, and so on.

You don't have to spend a lot of money on the prizes. Most of the time, the managers or owners who run these promotions barter for prizes. They'll collect gift certificates from other area merchants, especially those they've done cross-promotions with. These prizes have included video rentals, car washes, restaurant gift certificates, movie passes, free oil changes, CDs, books, small electronics, and so on.

At the end of the month, you tally up all the redemptions and award your grand prize. We've given away items including TVs, boom boxes, and other stuff, but the one prize that had the most impact was the one that cost the least: a day off with pay.

This simple contest is a lot of fun for your crew members. They get to provide their friends and acquaintances a really good deal at your business. Of course, you're getting the distribution of a printed piece that provides motivation for that new customer to come in. With ten employees averaging fifty pieces, you're getting five hundred individually distributed certificates. You should find a very strong redemption rate, given the unique method of distribution. Additionally, a piece that is personally handed out by an employee adds credibility to the program.

You'll probably find that there's one employee that does way better than everyone else. And it will probably be someone you least expect. One of the pleasant side effects of this promotion is that you identify an employee who really likes to market. This person can be a valuable resource for other marketing programs, including helping you set up more cross-promotions or supervising some of your community involvement activities.

CUSTOMER REFERRAL PROGRAM

Every businessperson will tell you that referrals are the best form of advertising. They certainly have the highest ROMI, since they cost you nothing. But you can't always rely on your customers to aggressively promote you as much as you'd like. So give them a little extra incentive to think of you when they are talking to their friends and acquaintances. Consider the health club that uses a referral program for all new members. When a person first buys a membership in a health club, karate school, yoga class, Lamaze class, dance school, or other self-improvement activity, that is the magical time when you are most likely to get referrals. You have a window of about two to four weeks, which is the time they're most excited. But instead of leaving their referral effort to chance, you make it easy for them.

With each new membership or student who signs up, the new member is given three referral cards good for one free week or two free classes. The member signs and dates the cards to authorize the free trial program for his or her friend. If the friend signs up for a full membership, the referring member gets a spiff. The health club would add a free month to the person's membership, while the karate club would give him or her $25. The cash seemed to make the bigger impact, but either method can work well. Unlike the employee referral contest, this is an ongoing promotion. If the member uses all three of the "buddy passes," he or she can get more.

The printed certificate is part of the program's success. You don't rely on your members, students, or customers to tell their friends to come in for a free class. That printed certificate or pass provides a tangible reminder of the referral program. When they give one to a friend, the friend then has a tangible reminder. And when that friend redeems the pass, you have a tangible way of tracking the results. Having them tell you "Joe sent me" just won't do the job.

You can even take this ongoing referral program and run a more aggressive contest with it, in a similar vein as the employee referral program. Trade prizes and get a nice grand prize. Put up posters to promote the contest.

With a slight modification, nearly any type of business can use the customer referral program. Our Mercedes salesman offered dinners for two at a very nice restaurant if we gave his card to someone who came in for test drive. This guy felt so strongly about the appeal of his product and his ability to sell it that he gave us the spiff just for access to the right people, whether they bought or not. Clothes, jewelry, greeting cards, insurance, and just about any other kind of business could benefit from an organized customer referral program. This is one of those promotions that is a must-have in any Street Fighter's war chest of tactics.

SUGGEST-SELL PROMOTIONS

Suggest selling is a simple and inexpensive marketing technique used at the time of a purchase to increase sales and profitability. It may be as simple as getting your counter people to say "You want fries with that?" But in the real world, it often takes a little more initiative to get your people to suggest that one extra item that is so critical to adding extra dollars to your bottom line. With the right approach, you'll discover that it is relatively easy to add 10 percent to 20 percent more to an existing sale or to get an existing customer to buy just one more item.

My all-time favorite example of the suggest-sell contest is the restaurant that, despite having really great banana cream pie, had very weak dessert sales. The owner ran a contest to motivate his servers to suggest dessert more aggressively. For one month, the server who sold the most banana cream pies would win one banana cream pie. And she would get to throw it in the owner's face! You never saw such a motivated crew in your life. The restaurant's dessert sales increased nearly 50 percent during the contest. After the contest, the residual effect was a 20 percent increase in dessert sales overall. Think about the return on investment from this one promotion. For the wholesale cost of one banana cream pie—and the cost of dry-cleaning one three-piece suit—the owner added thousands of dollars to the bottom line each week. And the side effect, of course, was that the crew had a great time with it. They didn't feel like they were being pressed to "push" something. They enjoyed it, and the customers responded as a result.

An ice-cream manufacturer in Canada wanted to promote its product more aggressively through a convenience store chain. The company offered to provide the chain with a contest enticing its employees to suggest the ice-cream bars at the cash register during a purchase. We suggested that the ice-cream company use a mystery shopper approach, where each store would be visited several times per month. If the employee suggested an ice-cream bar to the mystery shopper, that employee was handed a $50 bill on the spot. If the employee failed, that employee was handed a printed note telling him that he had just lost $50 but might get another chance. A contest like this creates excitement for employees, and as soon as someone wins some cash, the word spreads.

Suggest selling doesn't have to be limited to food items or contests. A good example from a service business is the approach we use in our own business. Once a client has booked one of us for a sales or marketing seminar at a meeting or convention, our salespeople offer to sell copies of our book *Street Fighter Marketing* in quantity for the attendees. When books are purchased as an add-on to a speaking contract, the client gets them for less than half the retail price. This happens about one-third of the time and generally adds about another 50 percent to the sale when it does. Those clients get a great price for the books, their attendees walk away with something tangible in their hands from the seminar, and we increase our sales.

To apply this to your business, identify a product or service that is high margin, low cost, and has broad appeal. Then give the customer a reason to buy that extra item on the spot.

A hardware store would up-sell lightbulbs at the counter. The cashier would inform the customer that the store is running a special on boxes of four lightbulbs: Buy one, get the second one half price. About half the customers would take advantage of the offer. The video rental store would do it with two-for-one boxes of candy. The quick-oil-change place did with 25 percent off air filters.

Once you figure out the item and the offer, you create a fun contest around it. You can use the mystery shopper approach, or you can give a prize for the most items sold. A major department store used a similar approach by giving its employees one giant Hershey's bar for each new credit card application taken. A department store credit card usually means that that customer would spend at least 10 percent more in the store. The cost of the Hershey's bars was a mere fraction of the total additional sales generated from each new cardholder.

REWARD PROGRAM FOR KEEPING APPOINTMENTS

Cancellations, no-shows, and short-notice changes in appointments can cost professional offices a lot of money. For a dental office, it's estimated that they cost upward of 30 percent of annual production, according to a leading practice consultant. That can translate to $130,000 of lost revenue in the average practice. So a $10,000 investment could show a significant return if it gets those patients to keep their appointments. That investment was used for a special patient reward program. Here's how it worked:

- The practice started promoting the program to patients six months in advance.
- Patients had to keep two consecutive regular checkup appointments.

- If they cancelled, rescheduled, or didn't show, they were dis-
  qualified.
- All eligible patients gathered for a year-end party.
- Their bill had to be current.
- The patients also had to follow the recommended treat-
  ment.
- A drawing was held for the winner of the grand prize at the
  patient appreciation party.

This was a win-win program for all because the patients received the care they needed, and the office generated more productive time in the schedule. Keeping the schedule full not only increased revenue from the regular checkups but gave the doctor an opportunity to diagnose problems that would have otherwise gone untreated. Again, the patient wins because more serious conditions are dealt with earlier, and the office benefits from increased production.

One Midwestern dental office, which allocated $5,000 for its grand prize, went from $30,000 to $48,000 in collections, and things are still improving. Even more impressive was the $10,000 grand prize used by the East Coast office that improved from $30,000 to $75,000.

To further enhance the value of the party, additional prizes were donated by other businesses whose owners just happened to be patients. Of course, it's hard to turn down a request for a free TV, trip, photography, or use of a time-share when the dentist is coming at you with the business end of a big drill.

The program, contest, and appreciation party were promoted with statement stuffers; promotional buttons worn by the staff; and, on display in the lobby, a three-by-six-foot Publishers Clearing House–style check made out to "Our Appreciated Patient." Also, when patients called to reschedule, they were told they could, *but* it would disqualify them from the grand prize drawing at the patient appreciation party later that year. It was estimated that at least two-thirds of the patients decided they didn't need to change their appointments after all.

Though designed specifically for dental offices, this type of contest could be used for any service business where you're selling time. Examples might include hair salons and providers of massage, chiropractic services, optical testing, cleaning services, lawn care, personal training, financial planning, accounting services, and on and on. One interesting result is that the patient who wins the grand prize often uses that money to get more dental work done that was not covered by insurance.

I'LL SHOW YOU MINE

Reciprocal Displays

This promotion is a little more involved, but under the right circumstances, it can effectively promote your key products to a strong target audience. Such was the case of the scuba shop that set up a display at a nearby travel agency. It cordoned off a small section near the front, where the agency was aggressively promoting cruises with great ports of call for diving and snorkeling. The scuba shop brought its showroom manikins fully dressed in wet suits, tanks, fins, and masks. The owner created a little display with other scuba paraphernalia and added some signage that offered a free scuba lesson to any person who signed up for a cruise.

That same display at the scuba store was fine for helping to interest people already considering scuba. But by moving that display to the travel agency, the scuba store dramatically increased its exposure to a new group of potential customers.

This approach can be used by any number of businesses: a grocery store and an appliance store; a Domino's and a home-theater store; and a makeup counter and a glamour photography service. It's a three-dimensional variation of a cross-promotion that can make a wonderful impact. Combine it with the distribution of the cross-promotional certificates to ensure that the visual has a takeaway piece that helps complete the sale.

Some doctors and dentists offices have a tropical fish tank because it helps to relax patients. If you have a pet store, you may want to provide the service of setting up the tanks and maintaining them in exchange for a sign that tells patients that your business is responsible for this tank. Also, make it part of the package that the office distributes cross-promotion pieces every so often; they could be good, perhaps, for a special deal on a starter tank. The same approach might also work for an upscale seafood restaurant.

INTERNAL SIGNAGE

Once someone is at your location, you have a number of different ways to communicate that cost very little money and take very little time. Use those opportunities to reinforce why the potential customer should buy from you. For example, if your business has a waiting room, provide some reading material that does more to position your business than some outdated copies of *U.S. News & World Report*. Testimonial letters or thank-you letters placed in a three-ring binder would make for some interesting reading while at the same time telling your customers how wonderful you are.

If you get some good positive publicity, have it framed and place it in your waiting area. Or better yet, have it enlarged to poster size. One orthodontist has a wall filled with patients' photos just after their braces are removed; this "success wall" is a great reinforcement to anyone inquiring about that procedure.

You can also use simple signs to help suggest sell additional items.

Another form of internal marketing is the "bag stuffer." Place a flyer or other type of promotional piece in the customer's bag to help you promote specific items. You can also use the bag stuffer as a form of promotional currency with another business. You place its promotional piece in your bags for your customers in exchange for its promoting your store.

A real simple message can be done on a three- to four-inch button worn by employees, which you can reinforce with the message on other signs and flyers in your location offering a special item.

You can really generate some word-of-mouth exposure by doing something totally outrageous from time to time. T. Scott Gross, a professional speaker who came out of the restaurant business, used a technique he calls "random acts of kindness." About once every quarter, without any advance notice, all the meals at this restaurant were free. When the customers came in that day, they had no idea it was going to happen. The return on investment was extremely high because the cost of those meals generated so much word of mouth that sales instantly increased in the following weeks. If you took that same investment in free meals and placed it in advertising, you would likely gain only a fraction of the new business.

To determine the best form of internal marketing for your business, try to walk into your business with a fresh look. Imagine what it is like for a first-time visitor. Where is his eye drawn? What does the environment do to make the customer feel comfortable about buying more? How do your people greet that customer? Even if one employee is busy helping someone else, she can glance over and acknowledge the person with a nod and perhaps gesture that she'll be there in just a minute. It's a little thing, but it makes people feel better about buying from you.

If you've seen magazine or newspaper articles that make consumers smarter about buying your products and services—and it also helps to reinforce the value you offer—have them enlarged and displayed. Have you won awards? Display the plaque or certificate and then some additional information to explain why winning this award is so significant.

One of the biggest annoyances that your customers have is waiting in line for service. Sometimes, this can't be helped. But you want to do everything you can to make that experience less frustrating.

Doggy Dog Promotion

One clever promotion was used by a burger franchisee from South Carolina. The owner came up with the idea "Dogs eat free." Of course, everyone has heard of promotions where kids eat free, but dogs got our attention. The employees collect the unused hamburgers that normally would have to be thrown out. They cut them up into bite-size pieces and give them to the customers' dogs when they go through the drive-through window. The promotion is done on a specific day of the week, and customers come by regularly to take advantage of it. The really clever part of the promotion is that it costs nothing. The restaurant doesn't have to buy treats, since it is using its own product.

Worst Seat in the House

One interesting promotion that turned a negative into a positive was written about by marketing expert Brad Kent.[13] The owner of a small café had one of his tables close to the door, and no one ever wanted to sit there. He decided to label the table "the worst table in the house." The person who sat there would save 50 percent on his entire check. Within a week, people in the neighborhood were talking about this café and the table they'd sat at last night where they got dinner for half price. There were some evenings when people would wait as long as forty-five-minutes to get that table.

Neighborhood Blitz

Bank branch managers are generally not the most comfortable in a selling situation. So one region of the Cincinnati-based Fifth Third Bank organized "neighborhood blitzes." Two branch managers would team up for several days. The first day, they would canvas businesses in the first branch's territory; the second day, they would do the same for the other branch. They would simply go door-to-door to small businesses, introduce themselves, and hand out a coffee mug with the bank logo it. When they got the ear of a decision maker, they would try to uncover what potential needs were not being met and see if there was interest in considering their bank.

8

INTER NET PROFIT

The internet can be an effective marketing tool for a local "brick and mortar" business. But since the internet, including your website, is just one of many different tools at your disposal, you want to ensure that a disproportionate amount of your resources are not tied up in one ever-changing marketing tool.

GETTING MORE VISITORS TO YOUR SITE

There are two main ways that potential buyers can find your website when they're searching for you using the main search engines or a browser. The link to your site will show either through a "sponsored link" or through an "organic search." A sponsored link, as the name implies, requires that you pay a fee to get the listing when a keyword is being searched. That fee is generally based on a Pay Per Click (PPC). The organic search is a little more complicated. The way you appear on a page of search results, or even *if* you appear, depends on a number of different factors relating to your website. The term for modifications made to a website to get higher on a list of search results is "optimization."

OPTIMIZATION

Natural search-engine optimization (SEO) of your website allows more potential buyers to find your site when they use a search engine. When a potential buyer conducts a search via a search engine (Yahoo, Google, MSN, among others), they enter some keywords or "key phrases." Your results in getting people to your website are directly related to your position on the results page when the search is conducted. According to the internet marketing firm 10X Marketing, "Those businesses that appear on the first page of these searches are getting 50 percent to 70 percent of the business from these

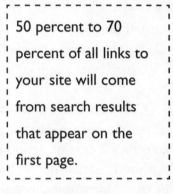

50 percent to 70 percent of all links to your site will come from search results that appear on the first page.

customers." For a company that depends on its website for a major portion of its business, appearing on page two instead of page one can mean literally tens of thousands of dollars a day in lost sales. Car rental companies and other travel related businesses, for example, know that the higher up they appear on the page, the more money they make.

To make sure they stay high up on the results listings, these types of companies turn to specialists that may cost thousands of dollars a month. For larger companies that rely heavily on their websites for purchases or reservations, it's well worth it. As the owner of a local company, you might be hard pressed to see a return on your investment, since you likely use your website as a supplement to your overall marketing efforts. Jason Harris of CeraNet (www.cera.net), a web-solutions company, is one of those specialists who suggest several simple modifications you can make to your site to get it to list higher during a search.

For the biggest return for the least amount of effort and cost,

Jason suggests the optimization effort be focused on the title bar, content, meta tags, press releases, submissions, and links. To see how this works, Jason had us select three keywords or phrases that we felt people might use in trying to find our company or our subject matter.

The three we chose were:

1. Jeff Slutsky
2. Neighborhood marketing
3. Guerilla marketing

Consider someone wanting to find a company that could help him with neighborhood marketing. That person would go onto Google or Yahoo and type into the search box: "neighborhood marketing." When Jason showed us these steps, *Street Fighter Marketing* showed up only as the fifth listing, but that listing was for an article we wrote for *Pizza Marketing Quarterly (PMQ)* magazine, and the link went to *its* site, not ours. It wasn't until the ninth listing that our alternate URL, www .streetfightermarketing.net, showed up. Even though we got two out of the ten listings on the first page, several alternatives were higher up. The higher up in the listings, the more likely you are to get potential customers to click through to your site. Placement on the page is critical.

For the best results, you want to appear as high up as possible on the page after a search. Better yet, it would be great if your company's listings made up the first five that showed up. This placement would help you bypass many of your competitors.

Given the weak response to our "neighborhood marketing" search, Jason made several recommendations of inexpensive changes to our website that would help to move us up in the rankings.

Title Bar

The bar is located along the top of a window or dialog box and displays the name of the window and/or software program being used. According to computer consultant Howard Eichenwald, the title bar is one of the main resources the major search engines use to determine the value of that web page to the search.

On our site, "Street Fighter Marketing, Inc." was the only string of words on the title bar of each page. Jason suggested that more relevant keywords should be in our title bar. That way it would be more likely for a page from our site to get selected for a given search. Therefore, if it's important for us to be found when there's a search for "neighborhood marketing," that key phrase should also appear on the title bar. In addition, you can maximize your title bar with other key phrases. Using this strategy, Jason changed our home page title bar to: "Street Fighter Marketing by Jeff Slutsky & Marc Slutsky—Guerrilla Marketing & Neighborhood Marketing."

On pages deeper in our website, we still had "Street Fighter Marketing, Inc." Since that phrase appears on the home page and in content throughout the site, we were not getting the maximum value from our various title bars. So we removed "Street Fighter Marketing, Inc." from all the pages other than our home page and added other keywords that we felt people would use when searching for the types of products and services that we offer.

Content

The next resource that the search engines look for, according to Jason, is content. The more there is, the better. One other key phrase that we wanted to use was "guerilla marketing," since many people use this as a generic term for local or neighborhood marketing. Marketing expert Jay Conrad Levinson did a brilliant job of branding the "guerrilla" series of books. Though our types of work are entirely different from Levinson's, the difference is not relevant from a search engine standpoint; many people looking for our type of service will use "guerilla" in their search.

With a "guerilla marketing" key phrase search, Street Fighter Marketing did not make the list for at least the first twelve pages. Since 70 percent of the action is on the first page, our goal was to get a listing as close to the first page as possible. To do this, we needed to use the phrase "guerilla marketing" in the content of our site.

We had several possibilities. First of all, our last book, *Street Fighter Marketing,* has a foreword written by Jay Conrad Levinson, author of *Guerrilla Marketing.* Levinson also gave us a quote for the cover of another one of our books, *How to Get Clients.* So Jason made sure that "guerilla marketing" was prominent in the description of those two products on our website.

Additionally, Jason added several pages of content about the subject "guerilla marketing." For six years, my brother Marc and I had written a weekly syndicated column for the Knight Ridder News Service. Consequently, we have a collection of over five hundred different articles. Several of them were about coauthors of Levinson's who wrote books in his "guerrilla" series. These included *Guerrilla Teleselling, Guerrilla Publicity,* and *Guerrilla Negotiating.* So these articles were added to the other articles on our website. Jason also suggested that we do quick rewrites in order to add "guerilla marketing" two or three times per page, as long as it made sense to each article. In this way, the search engines would be more likely to snag our site when a search for "guerilla marketing" was conducted.

Jason also warned that we shouldn't overdo it if we didn't want to be accused of "keyword stuffing" or "keyword spamming." Some people try to get more responses by mentioning a keyword twenty or more times in an article. Or some add those keywords a number of times using a font color the same as the background color so that the text does not show up but is recognized by the search engines. This is not advised, as it is possible for the search engines to blacklist you if you practice such an extreme approach.

Meta Tags

Meta tags are information placed in a web page not intended for users to see. Instead, they typically pass information to search engine crawlers, browser software, and some other applications. The most common meta tags relevant to search engines are keyword and description tags. Unlike normal HTML tags, meta tags do not affect how the page is displayed. Many search engines use information from meta tags when building their indices.

Meta tags are useful in providing your site with variations of keywords. There are a number of ways people might try to spell "Slutsky." To make it easy for the search engines to find your site, include every misspelled version of your keywords that you can use. For ideas, look at your junk mail. Those pieces will probably provide you with a good indication of the more common misspellings. For "Slutsky," I've seen: slutzky, slutski, slutzski, flutsky, slusky, lutsky, stutsky—and the worst one: shitsky. These are now appearing as meta tags. We have done the same with "guerilla," using gorilla, gorila, gurilla, guerrila, guerila, and so forth.

To begin the optimizing process for your website, your first step is to write down all the keywords and phrases that you think potential customers in the market for your products or services might use. Start with the obvious. When we searched for "Jeff Slutsky," our website was the very first listing. That was the good news. However, when we searched for "Slutsky," which could be the way many do search for us, though we showed up, it was a different story. You would think that Slutsky would not be that common of a name, and you would be right. In my Google search for "Slutsky," I discovered that it is the 78,019th most popular last name (surname) in the United States; the frequency is 0.000 percent; and the percentile is 89.455.[14] But as uncommon as it is, there are several other Slutskys getting more cyber attention than me. The list topper is Eugene (Yevgeni) Slutsky (1880–1948), a Russian economist who created something called the Slutsky Theorem. As far as my brother and I know, we're not related to Eugene. In any event, we do know that he has nothing to do with marketing. The famous Slutsky equation is: $(\partial X/\partial p_i)_y = (\partial X/\partial p_i)_u - x_i(\partial X/\partial y)_p$. I have no idea what the equation means other than that Eugene dominates the result pages. (If it wasn't for QuickBooks, I wouldn't even be able to balance my checkbook.) There are also a famous Russian poet named Boris Slutsky, a dentist in Philadelphia, a poster artist named Stan, and an intellectual-property lawyer in Atlanta. There are a few listings referencing us from speaker bureaus, but it's not until the second-to-last listing on the ninth page that a link to our website shows up. Thus, the challenge remains, how does Jeff Slutsky list higher when searched.

After you've created a list of keywords and phrases for your company, prioritize them. For our exercise, we chose three; however, the list could be much larger. But remember that each individual word and phrase will need its own list of actionable steps to optimize your results. Try to determine which ones are most likely to be used by your potential buyers to help them find a website that will mention your product or service. Go onto Yahoo, Google, and MSN, and search each of the words or phrases to see where you appear, if at all, in the results from the search.

Once you see where you are on the list, your efforts should go into moving your website up that list. Take the first keyword or phrase on your list and do the same three things that Jason did for us: First, add them to the title bar on your home page and all the other relevant pages in your site. Next, create some content about that subject. This content can be contained in an article. Use the keyword or phrase three times on each web page of the article. If your article is long, you can break it up into a number of different pages. (Each page should be around five hundred words). From a search engine perspective, two pages with five hundred words apiece are better than one page of one thousand words. Third, add that keyword or phrase into your meta tags, including all the misspelled or misused versions of the words or phrases that you're aware of. Ask yourself if there is a word or phrase that customers use when they have you confused with another site. Follow the same process for the second word or phrase on your list.

The first keyword on your list should be your company name. If someone is already aware of your business and simply wants additional information or a way to contact you, don't make it difficult for him to track you down. This is the low-hanging fruit, so pick it first. Then start to work your key product or services lines. Our baby brother, Howard, is a CPA. His keyword/phrase list should include: Howard Slutsky, CPA, accounting, accountant, taxes, tax refund, audit, and so on. He doesn't show high up in a search, especially combined with his geographical location (Columbus, Ohio; Gahanna, Ohio). That is why he needs to follow some of Jason's tactics to improve his position. After a while, Howard may discover that some of the words we chose aren't that valuable, and others are more important. This is a dynamic process, and you will need to make regular, perhaps monthly, updates.

Press Releases

Sending out press releases through the right sources can dramatically move you up in search results. Sending out your release through a service like PR Newswire will get your release looked at by numerous sites. Your release should be keyword focused. You may not get the media to do articles about you, but even so, sending out releases will help drive your site higher up in the order it appears in search results. Using the same keyword focus, you can run a campaign every month for four or five months. According to Jason, Tuesdays and Wednesdays are the best days for sending out these releases. In the example below, notice how many times the key phrase "neighborhood marketing" is used throughout the release. Jason also recommends that you add a paragraph at the end about your company, so that your web address is actually in the body of the release as opposed to the header in a traditional press release. Note: The key phrases that are underscored are to help illustrate the point and would not appear in the original release.

Submissions

Submission to the search engines and directories is very important to do at least once. Some people like to resubmit every so often, but that first submission is critical to getting the engines aware of your existence. There is some legwork involved, in that you have to go to each engine's site, find the form, fill it out, and submit it.

Links

One other way that search engines evaluate your site's relevance is by the number of other sites that point to yours. If a given site scores real high and also points to your site, there's a good chance that it will help improve your site's visibility. When possible, you might want to get reciprocal links to and from your site.

Street Fighter Marketing
800-758-8759
marc@streetfightermarketing.com
www.streetfightermarketing.com

FOR IMMEDIATE RELEASE

Neighborhood Marketing For Bigger Return on Your Marketing Investment

In the current hypercompetitive, advertising-polluted environment, you are paying more and getting less for your marketing dollar, according to Jeff Slutsky, president of Street Fighter Marketing, a training and speaking company specializing in neighborhood marketing. He went on to say, "This means it costs you more to attract customers than it used to." Yet you are likely putting the majority of your marketing dollars into some form of local mass advertising. The traditional advertising media has suffered from an erosion of its effectiveness. This downward trend is likely to continue.

To counter this downward trend, companies are now looking at local neighborhood marketing tactics to pick up the slack. But the problem with most neighborhood marketing programs is that they're too complicated and time intensive to implement on a regular basis. Slutsky suggested, "The Street Fighter Marketing approach to local neighborhood marketing teaches proven tactics that are easy to implement." Consider the fast-food unit that cross-promoted with a national video rental chain. The assistant manager was a restaurant customer three times a week. The entire promotion was set up at lunch, on-site, in five minutes. It generated over one hundred new customers. The return on investment was very high in both money and time.

About Street Fighter Marketing

Street Fighter Marketing was founded in 1980 by Jeff Slutsky and is based in Columbus, Ohio. It specializes in helping businesses learn how to market, advertise, promote, and sell using only a shoestring budget with neighborhood marketing and guerilla-style tactics, primarily through training and consulting projects, keynote speeches, and seminars, as well as a variety of Street Fighter training videos, audio programs, and books. For more information about Street Fighter Marketing, Inc., please visit www.streetfightermarketing.com.

Attack Plan

Consider the key phrase "motivational speaker." We don't consider ourselves "motivational" speakers as such, since we provide a lot of content in our talks. Still, that might be the phrase people use to research possible keynotes. To increase the likelihood of getting noticed by the search engines, we can:

1. Put the phrase "motivational speaker" in several of the title bars.
2. Add a couple of articles about "motivational speakers" on our site, with the key phrase mentioned three times in each page.
3. Where it makes sense, add the key phrase to other parts of our site in our descriptions.
4. Arrange reciprocal links to other motivational speakers' websites, especially those with a great deal of web visibility.
5. Add "motivational speaker" to the meta tags, including variations such as "motivational speaking" and "inspirational speaker."

Once you get someone to your site, your goal is to get that person to take some kind of action. With that in mind, you'll want to modify your website accordingly.

SPONSORED LINKS—PAY PER CLICK

Google, Yahoo, and other search engines provide an advertising service where interested surfers can go from their site to your site with a click. They charge you for each click. It sounds like a no-lose proposition, but if you're not careful, you could end up paying hundreds of dollars a month for this service. That would be fine, of course, if the cost generated a reasonable amount of new sales for you.

Dan has a poster printing and marketing company. He gets a fair amount of his business through his website. Using Google's AdWords and other similar programs, he increased the traffic and sales on his website. The problem was that the increase in sales did not cover the advertising cost. As in any type of marketing, you must use it wisely to make it worth your while.

We tried this method on our own. By googling "Jeff Slutsky," we saw that there were a number of sponsored links popping up from speaker bureaus. They were paying money to have access to people looking for me. It's great to have speaker bureaus aggressively marketing me, but if someone were looking specifically for me instead of a speaker on marketing, one of that person's choices should be us! So we started paying per click, so that if someone searches specifically for "Jeff Slutsky," we would be one of the first choices. We started to get charged a couple hundred dollars a month, and we weren't getting any actual bookings from it. We clearly didn't know what we were doing, so we dropped it.

YOUR WEBSITE

For most local businesses, the web can be a great additional tool. But it's just that: additional. Unless you have a full-blown e-commerce function and plan to do business all over the world, you need to focus your efforts on the web at a level that makes sense for you.

First of all, you *should* have a website. Many potential customers will want to look at your site before they call or visit you in person. In that regard, your site is more a "disqualifier" than anything else. That is, they'll look at your site to make sure you can solve their problem.

Therefore, you need a presence on the web, and it must be one that is good enough to do the job. It is possible to spend a small fortune on your website. For most small local businesses, a huge expense developing your site can't be justified based on the potential return. There are likely much more effective ways to spend your limited marketing dollars. So when planning your website, plan for something very simple that does the job and doesn't cost a lot of money.

Your web developer can probably use an existing template that allows you to plug in your elements. Make sure it's clean, easy to read, and provides the information you think your customers need in order to feel comfortable to contact you by email, phone, or fax, or to make a visit. Think of your website as an interactive brochure about your business. One of the biggest mistakes you can make is to let some technical parasite convince you to buy a much more elaborate site than you need. Here are some key issues to look for in your site:

1. As you are designing it, be sure to incorporate all the optimization tactics mentioned earlier.
2. You should be able to casily update information yourself. You don't want to have to pay someone every time that you want to make a simple copy change, add content, or add a photograph.
3. Make sure your home page loads quickly. Many sites feature bells and whistles to make it more interesting, like flash, a multimedia animation program developed by MacroMedia. The problem with flash is that it takes a long time to load, and most people don't have the patience to wait for the page to open. If you're going to use flash, video, or anything that takes time to load, it should be on deeper pages in your site.
4. Provide a printable version of your information. Make it easy for a prospective buyer to print out your information so that it can be read and used easily.
5. Have contact information on every page, making it easy for potential customers to call, email, or fax you. Don't make them look for "Contact Us" to find out how to get in touch with you.

6. Test the email addresses connected to your site. Make sure that everything works right, because if someone is sending you an email, and for some reason it's not getting to you, you may never know about it. It could be a lost opportunity. We suggest that you send yourself an email at least once a week to test your connections.

7. Decide how often you need to add or change things. Is it important for your site to bring the same customer back repeatedly? Or do you want a potential first-time buyer to feel comfortable enough to actually pay you a visit at your location? There's a big difference between the two objectives. The two different objectives require very different tactics. So think it through carefully! If you feel it is important to bring people back often, you're going to be spending a lot of time coming up with new content and reasons for them to visit you again.

8. Even if you don't have a lot of capability to make changes yourself, you might want to at least set up a few special pages that allow you to personally upload your information. These pages could include content as simple as weekly specials shown through photos and simple copy.

Now that you have a website, you need to get people to go to it. Just because you have one, doesn't mean you'll get traffic on it automatically. For a local business with limited marketing dollars available, you want to be very stingy on how you market your site. You have to make the decision to spend your marketing dollars to get people to your site or to your business.

Start with Free Exposure

Put your website address, or URL, on all the marketing and advertising pieces that you are using already. Wherever you would put your phone number, include your web address. This measure costs you nothing. Include the information on your business cards, letterhead, any media advertising, on the side of your trucks, and so on.

Beyond that, it depends on what type of business you have as to whether it makes sense to pay money to drive traffic to your site. Remember, if you're using your site as a supplement to your other marketing, it may not make sense to seek business on a national level by marketing your website directly. However, if you run a specialty business, or you're able to offer a unique value or service that people might not be able to purchase locally, then it might make sense. For example, after the birth of our triplets, my wife, Helene, started a business selling hand-made embellished hats  for infant girls. She started promoting her site through organizations for mothers of multiples. Her business is specifically e-commerce, so all of her marketing is geared to drive people to www.ridiculouslycutehats.com. Optimizing and sponsored links show her a strong ROMI compared to more traditional forms of advertising.

Monetizing Your Site

Jason recommended that we consider adding some links from our site to other sites that would pay us a commission for items sold. He called this "monetizing" our site. We were concerned that it might cheapen our site, and we'd lose credibility. However, we decided that if those links made sense in some way, it could be a big advantage to our readers.

Two opportunities came to mind: The first was a long-standing problem we had. Our current URL is www.streetfightermarketing.com. But our original URL was www.streetfighter.com. The original address was shorter and better, or so we thought. It also generated as many as 250,000 hits in a month. The problem we had was that the vast majority of the people coming to our site were boys inquiring about the Street Fighter video game. When they found out that we weren't the game, they were mad. We would get scathing emails from these kids because they thought we were taking advantage of the name. The fact was that we owned "streetfighter" long before Capcom created the game. At one point, the kids organized an attack on our site and forced us to crash. That was when we decided to add the word *marketing* to our URL.

Still, we own the original URL. And there are still some that search for us by that name.

Jason suggested that we create a banner link on our home page that basically says "If you're looking for the Street Fighter video game, click here." The link takes users to a listing of all the Street Fighter video games offered on Amazon.

Another link that makes sense for us is www.vistaprint.com, because some of our tactics involve the types of printing VistaPrint does, including business cards, invitations, greeting cards, and postcards. We use its services ourselves and have recommended the company to our clients as well. Using the link allows our visitors to qualify for free items.

In both cases, the money generated is like a small bonus for us, but the value to those people coming to our site is very strong.

For your website, determine if there are possible links that will provide your readers added value and, at the same time, give you the potential of earning a little extra money. You will want to make sure that any other URLs you refer users to make sense based on the type of product or service you provide. Also, be sure that your URL doesn't attract the wrong group because of confusion over the name. If it does, find out which sites they really want, and see if you can work out an associate relationship with those sites.

eBay

You can make money while you sleep by selling your unsold inventory on eBay, according to Helene Eichenwald, a successful Kansas City–based "e-tailer." Eichenwald points out several advantages of this approach for any kind of business with merchandise on the books:

1. It generates additional cash flow at little expense and with little effort.
2. It avoids conditioning your regular retail customers to wait for closeouts and major markdowns.
3. It expands your market globally.
4. It allows you to market using your off-peak times.

To be successful on eBay, Eichenwald has the following tips:

Use Multiple Photographs of the Product

You get one free photo, and each additional photo costs extra. Pay the extra. Show the item from several angles, especially all tags and original packaging. Since buyers can't see the product firsthand, you need to prove that it's new and in mint condition.

Use a Strong Title

You have a limited number of characters in the title, which is what most people search by. Use the most critical words. There are several well-known abbreviations: NIB (new in box) and NWT (new with tags). If the item is a brand-name product, put that in the title, as well as keywords that describe it. Include the regular suggested retail price.

Use a Detailed Description

Think of your item from your buyers' perspective. You want to use strong selling copy just like an ad or a catalog description would. Suggest ways the item can be used. When giving a feature, follow it with a benefit.

Make it Easy for Your Customers to Buy

PayPal, which is owned by eBay, allows the buyer to use a credit card or check, with the net payment deposited directly into your business checking account. When payment is confirmed, you'll receive an email, and you can ship the item.

Sell Brand-name Popular Items

The more the buyers are familiar with your products, the easier it is to sell. Remember, they will be comparing your offering to the same item at retail. To get an idea of how to set your minimum bid, go on eBay and search for similar items to see how they're priced and displayed.

Pricing

You may find that people who purchase items on eBay are very price sensitive. So you can expect to get a fraction of what you normally would get otherwise. Figure that into your pricing. You will also want to make sure the pricing is attractive enough to start the bidding. Hopefully, you'll have multiple bids that will run the price up. But if not, you should price it at a level that you don't mind selling at. Buyers will also look at the cost of shipping and handling. You can keep the initial price low with a more aggressive shipping and handling charge. The advantage of that is that your listing fee will be lower.

It's very important that you make good on any promises. If you get negative feedback from a buyer, you can't change it. People do look at your feedback score to see if they want to do business with you.

eBay Store

If you want to have e-commerce capability but aren't excited about putting up many thousands of dollars to build a website that can process orders, consider opening an eBay store. There's no or little up-front cost. You pay a fee every time something sells. It's easy to set up and easy to update. Simply have your URL point to your eBay store site. Even though eBay will take a cut from each sale, especially lower-ticket items, it's worth it if you want a low-risk way to get started. If your online business really starts to take off, you can always create your own website then. When my wife wanted a website for her infant-hat business, Jason suggested that she do it with an eBay store. Her URL points directly to her store, and she had an easy-to-modify e-commerce website up and running with no up-front cost.

9

PROFITING FROM NONPROFITS

One of the most exciting Street Fighter Solutions is generating new customers at no cost while at the same time helping local worthy causes raise money. And the best part is that these promotional opportunities literally knock at your front door. During the next several months, you'll no doubt be asked to donate money to some local cause. Many of these requests will come from your own customers. You may be asked to buy ads in their programs or to sponsor a local team. Each of these requests can have several outcomes. First, if you buy the advertisement or sponsorship, you will have very little, if any, ROMI. However, many of these are opportunities for you to convert their request into a major fund-raiser that will inexpensively bring you customers.

The big problem with most community involvement is that the events benefit the charity group but usually have very little benefit for the businesses that act as sponsors. They may get a little goodwill and exposure but very little tangible return. The Street Fighter Solution is to structure your various community involvement events so that your business generates new customers without a cost to you in either time or dollars. Within those parameters, you will show an incredible ROMI.

CHARITY DAY

We've been teaching our clients how to do this particular type of fund-raiser for many years. With every event, we've learned a little bit more about how to maximize the opportunity. If you follow these guidelines, you should be able to plan a successful fund-raiser that benefits *your* company.

Choose your nonprofit organization wisely. Make sure it is very motivated and well organized. Its members will have to do the lion's share of the promotional activity, and for the promotion to generate results, you want them out in your neighborhood aggressively getting the word out about this event.

Once you've identified a worthy organization that wishes to raise money for a worthy cause, you'll provide the means by which it does it. You will give the organization one day, with around four weeks' lead time. This should not be your company's best day or its worst day of the week. For most local businesses, this could be Tuesday, Wednesday, or Thursday.

You back out what your normal sales would be for that day. Be fair. Don't inflate the number. If you normally do $2,000 on an average Wednesday, then that's the number you tell to the group. After you get your $2,000 in sales, a portion of all additional sales will go to the organization. To make this work, you need to give it a significant amount. Generally, we suggest you just break even on the additional sales. A restaurant may be running roughly 50 percent on food, labor, and paper costs, so it would donate half of all sales in excess of the $2,000. A car wash, video store, and many other retailers probably work on similar or higher margins. Between 5 percent and 10 percent of sales will sound like you're trying to take advantage. As long as you're accounting for your normal sales, you have nothing to lose by giving the nonprofit your entire markup on the additional sales.

The reason for backing out your break-even point is so that the organization knows it will make nothing if its volunteers don't aggressively pursue customers. It also allows you to maintain your normal sales for the week.

Feel free to offer ideas on how the nonprofit can promote the event, but make sure it provides the footwork. Have the member talk to a local quick printer to get flyers, posters, banners, and yard signs donated. Then have them organize a community blitz, where they distribute all those promotional pieces. Suggest that they contact the local news media to announce the event, including the daily and weekly papers, radio, and TV stations. They may even be able to get a free billboard or two if there is some unused inventory available. They can also approach local merchants who have marquee signs and ask them to promote the event on their signs for a week. At this point, you've received a great deal of free exposure in the neighborhood. But this exposure is just an extra benefit.

Starting perhaps a week or less before the promotion, feel free to promote it to your own customers. You can put it up on your own marquee, use a banner, hand out flyers at your register, and so on.

On the day of the event, plan on a much larger amount of foot traffic. Make sure you have plenty of product and labor to handle the increased customer count. Have the organization decorate your location inside and out to make it look like a special event. In some situations, the organization can provide you with extra labor.

The bounce-back certificate is a simple but often overlooked element of this type of promotion. You create a printed piece on behalf of the organization. I usually like to use a half-sheet

(8½" x 5¼"). It is written from the point of view of the non-profit group and says something like "Thank you for supporting our event. Bring this certificate back within the next two weeks and buy any _____ at the regular price, and $_____ will be donated to our cause." This helps ensure that any first-time customers the event generated become repeat customers. It also helps you increase the total amount of the donation to the organization at no cost to you. The bounce-back certificate usually has the value of an aggressive coupon, but instead of the discount going to the customer, its value goes to charity.

> The *bounce-back certificate* is the most forgotten piece of a successful community fund-raising event.

Now let's look at this event from the Street Fighter's perspective, with a keen eye on the ROMI:

1. First and foremost, this type of promotion generates new customers. People come to your business and try the product or service. In addition, many of the first-timers will come back again later.

2. Second, it doesn't cost you anything out of pocket. You back out your normal average sales for that day, making sure that the donation doesn't impact your bottom line. In addition, it provides the proper incentive for the volunteers to actively promote the event.

3. Third, it takes very little of your time. You organize the event so that the volunteers do all the work. You simply run a normal (albeit slightly higher volume) operation and provide the means that they need to raise money. But you ensure that the nonprofit group conducts its grassroots marketing campaign to get the local citizenry to support the event and the cause.

4. The opportunity comes to you. You don't have to knock on doors to set up the promotion. You can also put up a poster at your business that tells your customers that you support a wide variety of community causes and to ask for details.

5. The new customers that were generated were not motivated to try you *because of a discount*. They paid full price. Money was donated to the cause from the purchase, but the regular-price integrity was maintained.

The return on investment for these types of events is usually extremely high. In one such event with a local Pizza Hut, there were an estimated fifty new customers eating there for the first time, and about half of them became regulars. Since the restaurant's average regular customer is good for about $2,000 per year, this one promotion could be responsible for $50,000 in new sales. And since the actual cost to the Pizza Hut was nil, the return was very high. All the goodwill, PR, and flyers were just icing on the cake.

One last fine-tuning element is to do a fishbowl drawing. This drawing requires participants to provide their name, address, phone, and email. Capturing these names is important because you can expect a lot of new faces at the event. So in addition to doing a bounce-back, you can also do an inexpensive postcard mailing or an email message with the same offer a few weeks later as a reminder.

This exact format has been used by a number of local businesses successfully. One key issue is to make sure that the opportunity is right for you. As I suggested earlier, when considering a fund-raising event like the one just described, make sure the organization is well organized and motivated to promote the event. Don't assume that its volunteers know how to get the word out. Be prepared to give the group some direction, to make sure you get a good turnout. These methods include distributing flyers and posters, getting mentions in the media, the use of signage, and so on.

Your fund-raiser needs to be performance based. That is, you donate money only after you've generated a sale. Backing out your normal sales lets the group know that it will have to hustle to make money. Also, if the cause and the organization are local, your response is likely to be better. You want to be the dominant donor for this cause in your community.

A similar program was conducted by a casual-dining restaurant after one of its crew members was tragically killed in an auto accident. Her parents, via the obituary, requested that all contributions and memorials be made to the Special Wish Foundation. With permission from the parents, the manager designated a Tuesday where half of all proceeds above the restaurant's normal average sales would be donated. He determined that his average Tuesday sales were $5,891, so he set the goal of generating $7,891, which would provide for a $1,000 donation.

On a volunteer basis, crew members distributed flyers and posters, plus they collected items from local merchants for a raffle. Some crew members got local bands to play in the parking lot that day to add to the event. The manager created and mailed a press release to all media outlets within thirty miles. Lastly, they provided bounce-back certificates to all the guests that supported the event. Again, "bounce-backs" are internal coupons designed to motivate a return visit.

The press release resulted in a radio station providing a two-hour live remote broadcast. Plus, they received numerous mentions on several radio stations and all three TV network affiliates.

Most businesses would evaluate the success of such an event based on the thousands of dollars' worth of free advertising exposure they received. This exposure is definitely good. But what did the event do for actual sales?

The restaurant took in $9,819 for a day on which the average is $5,891. Its weekly sales increased 10.35 percent over the previous week. These are tangible, traceable numbers.

We were very pleased with this manager's effort. He created a Street Fighter Marketing Solution out of an internal opportunity, while providing a valuable service to the local community. The only enhancement we would have suggested with this promotion was to make the bounce-back certificate good for both a small discount and an additional donation to the cause. So, instead of a $5-off coupon, it would have been a $2.50 discount and a $2.50 donation. Then track the results. The bounce-backs would tell you how many people came to the event and were likely to become regular customers. That's where the most significant potential returns lie.

When we see companies do similar types of promotions, they often really miss the boat in several key areas. Frequently, they use their own advertising money to promote the event. They don't get the organization to actively promote it for them. They pick causes that may be too broad in nature or too specific to the community. And they often don't make the fund-raising performanced based. Without these elements, the promotion is just a PR fund-raiser. In contrast, a Street Fighter Solution, in addition to the PR value, generates actual return-on-investment results. There are little differences in the program structure, but the differences in outcome are huge in nature.

Once you get the hang of this type of promotion, it's something you can plan to do every two to three months if you have enough qualified opportunities to support it. It's good to have one or two really good organizations that allow your business to host annual events.

Charity Coupon Distribution

Sometimes the onetime event is not right for a given organization. You can offer to provide those organizations with special coupons to be redeemed at your business. But instead of a discount going to the user, the value of the coupon goes the organization. In this way, you get a highly visible local organization approaching members of the community and handing out your coupons. Its volunteers verbally encourage community members to go to your place of business and use the coupons in order that their organization can receive the donation.

There is no cost to you except for printing the coupons. Because you make a donation only when you get an actual sale, there's no risk. This approach is particularly attractive to businesses because they donate money only when they get a paying customer. This approach works particularly well with businesses that sell high frequency, low-cost items such as food, movie rentals, CD sales, and so forth. You give the organization's volunteers one week to hand out coupons with a thirty-day expiration date on them.

The Endowment Enhancement

You don't have to be a retailer to do this type of community outreach program. The same basic format has been used by quick-oil-change units, sewing machine dealers, computer retailers, and even life insurance agencies.

Consider David, the owner of a life insurance agency. I was very impressed when he organized a fund-raiser to help the endowment of his temple. His company created a special life insurance policy with the temple as the beneficiary. The temple's goal was to raise an additional $1 million for its endowment. Each individual policy would have a $10,000 payout at death. This meant that David needed to sell one hundred policies to reach their $1 million goal. The cost of the policy was eleven annual premiums ranging between $119 and $430 per year, depending on the congregant's age. It was made clear that the agent commissions on these sales were donated back to the cause, so there would be no hint of duplicity. David kicked it off by buying the first ten units. He then listed the most generous congregants and suggested that they, too, buy ten units each. His objective was to get the congregation's "heavy hitters" to cover half of the $1 million goal.

This program would not have a very good short-term ROMI because of the time commitment required for such a small amount of commissions. But if you look at these fund-raising policies as kind of a loss leader, the long-term ROMI could be great.

Think about how much time and money it would take David just to get in front of all of these people specifically to talk about his product. This fund-raising opportunity allowed him to have access to a very beneficial target audience willing to discuss his product. He then could establish a rapport and build relationships that would translate into profitable policies later on.

Trade-in Sales

Another approach to community involvement would be to serve as a collection point for items needed for the less fortunate in your community. However, you can tie the donated items into a new sale. So instead of just running a sale and lowering the price to attract buyers, use the used item as the reason for the discount. For example, a local optometrist can offer a special discount on a new pair of glasses when a customer trades in an old pair. The organization gets the word out about the promotion, and the optometrist collects the old glasses, which are then donated to the organization. The same has been done with winter coats, shoes, books, computers, and even canned goods.

This approach allows you to better maintain your price integrity. You are giving your customers a legitimate reason for lowering your price. It also allows you to be a contributor to your community at a minimal cost. That cost is usually in the form of making sure that the donated items are in decent working condition to be useful.

Bundling Your Service

Service businesses that sell low-ticket items can participate in fund-raising through the donation of gift certificates. One of our clients, a pizza chain, offered a pizza a month for one year as a grand prize in a local high-school fund-raiser. This prize had a face value of $150. Out-of-pocket cost to the restaurant was about $50, without taking into consideration the fact that the winner was likely to buy beverages, salad, and more when he or she came in to get the monthly pizza. The same was done with a full-service car wash that provided a premium wash once a week for a year. That prize was worth nearly $700.

Provide the Venue

Non-profit organizations don't hesitate to approach businesses to ask for their help by making their office or store the site for an event or to propose a value-added, savings, certificate, or sponsorship program. Getting involved can provide a business with an opportunity to attract new customers and make a profit while at the same time generating money for a good cause.

Car washes, bakeries, and candy shops are just some of the several types of businesses that could lose business to fund-raisers. Rather than take the risk, open your business up to fund-raising. Instead of cheerleaders washing cars in the parking lot of a local Taco Bell, provide them access to your car wash. They promote—and they dry. You provide the bounce-back certificate. They want to sell baked goods, and you run a bakery or donut shop; let them sell *your* baked goods.

The Charity Auction

The charity auction works well for charities and for businesses. The nonprofit organization asks local businesses to donate their products and services to the auction and then promotes the event. The business gets exposure in the program book and from the attendees at the event. A business can often donate quality items that may not have been great sellers. It's a good opportunity for attendees to pick up some bargains while raising money for a worthy cause.

A silent auction is also a very popular and productive fundraising event for many organizations. Not only is it a good idea to support worthy causes by donating your products or services, but if you do it right, you can get great exposure for your business. Of course, the big advantage of participating in a silent auction is that you're not donating hard dollars even if your product does cost dollars. Keep in mind that many of your potential customers attend these events, so you will want to look for ways to get the most out of your efforts.

Most businesses generally donate one or two items to an auction. However, some of the most popular offerings are those that provide a much higher total value. One example is the salon that donated one facial a week for a year. Depending on the type of business you're in, you can really build value by packaging a number of your items into a weekly or monthly item that the winner receives for a year. This approach would also work easily with things like video rentals, car washes, food items, and so on.

Many businesses offer items that are left in inventory or are no longer popular. While on the surface it may make sense to unload this inventory for a worthy cause, from a marketing point of view, you're not getting your bang for the buck. Consider, instead, offering your most *popular* items. Remember, many people at these events will be exposed to your business name and learn what you do. You want to make sure that the participants associate you and your business with the products and services you want them to buy.

Once you commit to offer a collection of products and services that have a significant retail value, leverage your donation by negotiating with the emcee to give you many live mentions during the event. This request was made by a jewelry store that donated a $1,000 necklace. As part of the arrangement, the event agreed to mention the company and its offering ten times over the microphone and to direct people to the jewelry store's display.

At some smaller events, there may not even be a program. If there is, it may not contain advertising. Offer to print a program for an auction, listing all the items, in exchange for your ad on the back cover. This would be a doubly perfect opportunity for a printer. If the organization sells tickets to its silent auction, you can offer to print the tickets. Furthermore, to help sell tickets, you can offer to put an offer on the back of the ticket that creates additional value. If the tickets cost $25, you could offer $25 off the purchase of $100 or more at your business. It gives the impression that each person that buys a ticket gets his money back. Plus, you have now created an impression on everyone who attends the event—even before it happens.

Start Looking for Opportunities

Like cross promotions, you can set up your community outreach and fund-raising programs without leaving your location. Let the opportunities come to you. First, no doubt you have all kinds of solicitations from the local community. When approached about a donation, ask a lot of questions. See if there is potential to build a simple request into a full-blown fund-raising promotion. This is one time you'll want to wait for just the right kind of opportunity.

The other way to generate opportunities is to advertise in your location. With just a well-placed poster or other signage, you can let your customers know that you have the ability to help them raise money for worthy causes.

Tours of Your Business

It's always nice to open your doors to your community. School tours of your facility are an inexpensive way to foster a sense of goodwill in the community and to make a contribution. As good as that sounds, a Street Fighter Marketing Solution would require you to take that common idea and add one little element. Everybody who goes on the tour, when they leave, gets a special certificate to take home. It should be good for some kind of discount or value added on their next visit—plus an equal amount to be donated to the school's PTA or PTO. That little piece of paper is what provides the incentive for someone to become a customer after his or her child has just had a tour. It's also the way you'll track the results of your efforts.

Event Sponsorships

If you're going to invest in becoming a major sponsor of a local event, you will want to structure the sponsorship package in a way that will allow you a strong ROMI. Most sponsorship packages give you a little exposure in the media by placing your company name on T-shirts and through media coverage at the event. You want more. Think of all the possibilities that this organization can provide you that will bring customers into your business with little or no cost or effort. Sponsorship is no longer a matter of hanging your banner, getting a bunch of seats on the fifty-yard line, and meeting the star players. Sports and special events are now part of the marketing mix and are expected to deliver. Here are some basic ideas that can be used singly or combined in any number of ways that will help you achieve marketing success.

Bounce-backs—Use something at the event to bring the attendees to your store. For example, let the attendees know that they can bring in their ticket stubs and redeem it for one of your products. Or, at the event, give the attendees a coupon that is a special offering and is redeemable after the event.

Buy One, Get One Free (BOGO)—Taken alone, this is a product sale enticement. If combined with one of the other elements of sales promotion, it could increase product sales while also tying in with your event sponsorship. For example, as part of the BOGO promotion, you could provide a sweepstakes entry form for a free trip, free tickets, and so forth.

Contests/Sweepstakes—You can have registration at the point of purchase, at the event, and even through the mail. One word of caution: Don't undertake a contest without consulting a lawyer, since each state has very specific rules about entry requirements, probability-of-winning clauses, and so on.

Coupons—These can be either pre-event or at the event. If they are distributed through a retail facility, they can be used to promote your sponsorship before an event and, hopefully, to drive additional traffic to the event. In fact, the coupon could be distributed through your retail partner and used for event admission discounts. Or, coupons can be distributed at the event to drive sales after the event.

Database Development—As more and more companies get involved in marketing directly to their customers, take advantage of generating a list of your customers' names. Have a booth at your event where people can participate in a survey, enter a contest, or just register to win one of the hourly drawings held at the event.

Discounted Sales—Taken alone, they're a way to drive traffic into a store. Combined with a coupon or bounce-back, they are a way to reward an event attendee with an additional bonus for attending that event. Then combine it with a "register to win" promotion, and you not only measure the results of attendance at your sponsored event, but generate names for your database.

Free-standing Inserts (FSIs)—These can combine coupons, register-to-win promotions, sweepstakes, contests, and so on. They are the four-color advertising-only inserts that are so prevalent in your Sunday paper.

Hang Tags—There are literally tags that hang off the product. They can be used with soft goods and food products, particularly bottled beverages. Again, design the tag like a coupon to drive traffic to the event or like an entry form that provides an opportunity for its holder to win tickets to the event.

Internet—The entire cyberspace concept is wide open for sales promotion ideas. Special pre-event offers or discounts can be provided, as well as additional sponsor/event information that would entice customers to the event and encourage them to purchase your product.

Media Coupons—These are included in coupon mailings, newspapers, and magazine ads, as well as provided through other print-coupon distribution. Again, use them like coupons or bounce-backs to enhance pre- and post-event sales and participation.

On-air Promotions—Using radio, television, and cable, you can make the same offers as you would with coupons, only using the electronic media.

On-pack Promotions—Special offers on the product package can either be cut out or easily peeled off, and are similar to coupons and bounce-backs used to generate pre- and post-event coverage plus database development.

On-site Sampling—Use your sponsorship to introduce consumers to a new product through sampling. This can involve allowing consumers to taste a product or giving them a demonstration. Combine this offer with bounce-backs and/or register-to-win promotions, and you will have additional sales, as well as the opportunity to develop a potential customer database.

Point-of-purchase Tie-ins—These can consist of instant coupons at the checkout counter, on-shelf promotions, end-cap displays with "take one" tear pads, and so forth. Again, combine with some of the other sales promotion ideas to enhance results.

Point-of-purchase Promotions—These can include product sampling with coupons, point-of-sale promotions, contests, and so on. And point-of-purchase promotions can be at your retail partner's location before the event or at the event itself.

Product Promotions—These can include on-pack coupons or entry forms, register receipts with UPC codes, or any other form of promotion that is specific to proof of purchase. As with contests, check with your lawyer on the exact wording and application to ensure that you are not violating the law.

Product Sales—Very simply, sell your product at the event! This is a viable sponsorship benefit that allows you to add one of the other promotion ideas to measure impact and effectiveness such as coupons, bounce-backs, register-to-win promotions, and contests,.

Hole-in-one Contest—You can be a big hero in your community by putting up a prize valued at between $10,000 and $25,000 if someone gets a hole in one at the local charity golf event. According to US Hole In One,[15] you can insure just about any contest at any event. What would it cost you to put up such a huge grand prize? Depending on the amount of the prize and the difficulty of the task, between $200 and $400. For not a lot of money, you can own that event.

US Hole In One also suggests that you'll get more bang for your buck if the grand prize is your product instead of cash. Car dealers can put up a car for the contest. The car is out there at the event drawing interest. But if someone wins, it will cost the car dealer only several hundred dollars. Homebuilders use this as a way to give away a house. One gasoline company put up a grand prize of fifty thousand gallons of gas, but because of the rising price of gas, it wanted to limit its liability.

The prizes are not limited to golf events. You can buy insurance for half-court basketball shots, three strikes in a row at baseball events, football field goals, and so on. One of the more interesting promotions was Taco Bell's offer to give everyone in the stadium free tacos if slugger Barry Bonds hit a home run and the ball hit a specific target outside the stadium.

ÜBER OUTDOOR ADVERTISING

A brief history. Outdoor advertising is probably the oldest medium in the world, according to Ivan Vatahov.[16] Around 15,000 BCE the first messages that were the closest thing to outdoor advertising were discovered in caves. Perhaps some industrious hominid was running a sale in stone axes. Egyptian merchants used roadside stone tablets to promote their merchandise some three thousand years ago. Fast-forward a few hundred years or so and Grecians used wood-carved columns called *axones* to inform the spectators of the scheduled events at their games.

Around six hundred years ago bill posting was growing in popularity as an inexpensive marketing tool. "In 1796, came lithography, which facilitated the development of aesthetic qualities in advertising design. According to Henderson and Landau, by 1870, technological advances in mechanization had greatly improved poster art. Machines were invented for paper folding and cutting and printing and production of lithographic halftones. Under the guidance of such men as French artist Cheret, the look of advertising underwent a change with the use of color in modern posters."

Posters were a leading advertising method in the late eighteenth and early into the nineteenth century. These marketing pieces were produced in a variety of sizes and shapes. The copy on the posters got more sophisticated and even used celebrities of the day to endorse the products or special events like a circus. According to Neil C. Cockerline, "The circus also invented the concept of saturation advertising, often posting in cities with 50 to 100 standard sized billboards, 15,000 to 20,000 poster sheets, or the equivalents of 626 to 833 standard billboards."[17]

That was then. Now outdoor advertising is as varied as any medium and provides both some unique advantages and some unique challenges.

VEHICLE ADVERTISING

You can get free advertising exposure with your vehicles. Being clever with it will get you even more attention. Driving around town can be one of your best forms of advertising, according to Jeff Whiting of Help! Wizards, a Columbus, Ohio–based computer consulting firm that makes house calls. In October 1999, the company bought its first vehicle. Instead of going with a white van, as its owners had originally thought, 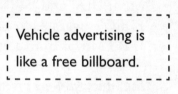 they decided to buy something that would attract more attention. So they bought a bright yellow Volkswagen Beetle. Their "Help! Wizards" logo is boldly blazoned on both sides of the bug, and their trademark exclamation point is on the hood. They've since added three more bugs to the fleet and have two more scheduled to hit the streets very soon. And the results? According to Whiting, they get at least one call a week directly from the exposure of the "Wizard Bug."

And speaking of bugs, an independent extermination company in Fort Wayne, Indiana, used an old hearse with a big bug on top as its vehicle. It got a lot of attention, but many customers felt uncomfortable with the hearse in their driveways.

If you would prefer to make your point more subtly, consider getting promotional vanity tags for your car. The right message can generate some interest. The plates that seem to make the most impact are the ones that take a few moments to figure out. They engage the reader, and then, once the plate's meaning is finally decoded, the reader remembers it forever. Here are some tags that we've seen or that have been submitted to us:

- "MR 2TH" (we assume he is a dentist).
- "I SUE 4 U" from a lawyer in California.
- "1099" or "W 2" is what we suggested to our CPA brother, Howard Slutsky.
- "401K" for an investment advisor specializing in retirement accounts.
- "BUYLOW" for a stock broker.
- "P8NTR" (we guess he is a painter).
- "MNIPUL8" and "SPINE" are from chiropractors.
- "EIEIO" suggested to a farm co-op manager.
- "U P 4 ME" is from a urologist in New Orleans.

One time, we were giving a keynote speech, and an audience member told us about the man who had one delivery vehicle. A friend of the man's, who had a large fleet, made fun of his single truck. So the man had some magnetic signs made with his company logo on it. Underneath the logo, on the left side, he put "Delivery Vehicle #1." "Delivery Vehicle #2" was placed on the right side. And on the back was "Delivery Vehicle #3." His friend was amazed at how fast his fleet had grown.

When considering signage for your vehicles, don't forget to include the left side, the right side, and the back. Also, if you do create a moving billboard with your vehicles, it must be very clear to your drivers that they have to drive courteously no matter what. Even a justifiable flipping off of a road-rage-ravaged cell-phone-talking lane hog can create a great deal of negative ill will and bad word of mouth.

For temporary vehicle signs, consider the use of vehicle magnets. They can have a very big impact—in full color if you want. This method would be a great way to promote something that you did not want to be on your vehicles permanently. You could even run monthly or seasonal specials using this approach. For example, a heating and cooling company could produce magnetic signs that promote preseason maintenance of customers' furnaces or air-conditioners. The signs would be used during the slower time leading up to the busy season when the weather changes.

If your company is sponsoring a local sports team or league (which is covered in another chapter), in addition to the normal exposure you get on the jerseys and the signage at the playing field, make it part of the deal that all the parents have to use your window decal in the back of their cars. Since parents usually have bumper stickers or window decals for the sport, anyway, you might as well provide them and make sure they include: "sponsored by [your company]." In this way, you will have dozens, if not hundreds, of cars providing you additional exposure at no additional cost. This strategy extends your exposure beyond the group itself and may be the tipping point for justifying your sponsorship with respect to ROMI.

With digital printing capabilities, graphics for vehicles can be very dramatic. Several of the most dramatic examples came from Germany on semitrailers. These optical illusions are super attention grabbers (see the following two pages). The only other element to consider is whether they provide a strong enough selling message to justify their cost. The two beverage examples seem to do a better job of it than the other two.

Your vehicles are moving billboards, and except for the cost of creation and application, your message is distributed free. Of course, if you're going to use your vehicles in this way, make sure that they are always clean. And, when not in use, park them in a high-traffic area, if possible, so they will still provide you additional free exposure.

YARD SIGNS

While researching the home improvement industry for a keynote speech to the National Association of the Remodeling Industry (NARI), I came across the fact that 75 percent of remodeling jobs came as a result of the yard signs used by remodeling companies at their job sites. All other forms of marketing combined didn't even come close. These inexpensive and, in many cases, disposable signs have the power to grab the attention of potential buyers. One reason seems to be that the sign shows that the company is doing the work for a neighbor. It's a form of referral and credibility. If the same sign was planted at a busy corner, it might not have the same impact, even though the traffic count was significantly higher. While consulting with Curb Light Appeal, a residential landscape lighting and design company, I told the owner, Eddy, about those stats. He ordered yard signs for his business, and, sure enough, they generated qualified leads.

Getting permission from the customer is key to using the signs. One way to work it in is to make it part of the deal that the customer must let you display your yard sign during the job and for fourteen to thirty days following completion. The customer is likely to be willing to comply, especially if asking for some kind of price consideration. You can even bump your prices a little in anticipation of the customer asking for a discount. When you quote the job, you can say, "The regular price is X, but if you let us display our yard sign for thirty days, we will knock five hundred dollars off the price."

Since yard signs are very small, it's important to make your message painfully simple. One element should say what is being done. Another element is the phone number. It could be something like:

Another Livable Basement by

JEFF - *THE*
BASEMENT
MAKER

CALL

800-758-8759

Pay the extra money to have the signs printed on both sides. Use a simple, easy-to-read typeface and high-contrast colors for the background and the lettering. When placing the sign, make sure that it's in a spot that is easy to read by passing traffic. For a corner home, you will want two signs, one for each direction.

Yard signs work only for those types of services that "improve" the home. You would not likely get permission if you were marketing bug extermination, leaky basement repair, toxic waste removal, or anything that requires a level-three hazmat suit or forces your house to be sealed in plastic like at the end of *E.T.*

BILLBOARDS

The granddaddy of outdoor advertising are billboards. They make an impact, no doubt. It can be a very creative medium. The only issue in question is if you can buy your billboards at a price that will get you a good return. Billboards can be expensive. If you don't have a high-visibility location, a billboard can help direct traffic to you. But for bringing in paying customers, is your money better spent elsewhere? The only way to know for sure is through trying and tracking. Sometimes the price of the boards is negotiable, and sometimes they're not. Plus, you have

BRADFORD W. BAKER'S FORMULA

FOR CALCULATING OUTDOOR RATES

READ

- Consider a 15-second read the standard.
- For a read between 20 and 29 seconds, add 5 percent.
- For a read of 30 seconds or longer, add 10 percent.
- For a read of 10 seconds or less, deduct 10 percent.

SIZE

- Deduct the actual square-foot percentage down from 14' x 48' (672 square feet).
- Example: If board is 12' x 28' (336 square feet), then it is 50 percent of the standard size (336/672), and its CPM should be 50 percent of the baseline CPM.

SIDE OF INTERSTATE

- Assumes right-hand read.
- If left-hand read, deduct 25 percent.

OBSTRUCTIONS

- If there are visual obstructions, like trees or poles, deduct 10 percent.

CIRCULATION

- Ultimately, you're after a target CPM based on DEC (Daily Effective Circulation, which should be supplied by the outdoor company).
- With each board, you'll need to start with this initial figure, then deduct the factors listed above to arrive at what it's worth to you.

to consider the cost of production. Currently, the standard is to produce your message on vinyl, which could cost you as much as a month or more of what the board itself will cost.

Location is important as well. Usually, the billboard companies price their boards on what they call a Gross Rating Point

(GRP) showing. This term is not directly related to the GRPs used in broadcast advertising.[18] What you want to find out is the AADT (Annual Average Daily Traffic). This is the total number of vehicles passing the location within twenty-four hours, based on counts taken over an entire year. As in broadcasting, you can figure out your CPM (Cost Per Thousand) based on the relationship of the AADT to the price.

Also, always do a pre-ride. Drive by each location you're considering to evaluate the *approach*. This is the distance measured along the line of travel from the point where the billboard first becomes fully visible to the point where the copy is no longer readable. See if there are any obstructions that may cut down on the visibility of your board. If it's winter, anticipate the leaves that will be on a nearby tree in spring. If it's summer, anticipate an earlier sundown in the fall, which may affect the number of drivers that see it on the drive home from work. Are those boards lighted, and if so, at what time are the lights set to come on? Drive by the locations during rush hour in each direction. See how much time people are spending at each location. Are they driving into the sun and therefore not seeing your board? Is traffic flow unencumbered, allowing drivers less time for looking at billboards? What else at each location competes for the driver's attention? It could be other boards, signage, displays, scenery, and so forth. As long as you're going to make a sizable investment, it's best to know exactly what you're getting for your money.

If you can't get the billboard company to come down on the price, see if it has some not-so-desirable locations that it's having trouble selling (usually in nonelection years). To create additional exposure, ask for some bonus boards. But you will want them after your main campaign is running so that you can use the existing vinyl instead of paying for extra. Also, note what you can do with the vinyl after the advertising campaign is over. It could make a very interesting backdrop for a trade-show booth, or perhaps it could be installed on the side of your building, if permitted.

A billboard salesman once gave me the idea of buying a billboard every other month for a year. The twelve consecutive months were good for a 10 percent discount. But buying only six months total would save 40 percent; it's likely that at the end of each month, you'll get free days or even weeks, since they may not change the board immediately. Once I got a total ten and a half months for the price of six. It may not always work, but it is a Street Fighter tactic to keep in mind for the right occasion.

More elaborate versions of billboards are wallscapes and spectaculars. Wallscapes are advertisements painted directly on building walls. Some walls can accommodate vinyl facings that are secured in a frame. Both have large-scale exposure and high visibility to vehicular and pedestrian traffic. They are generally geared for high-density areas like downtowns. Spectaculars are usually larger than fourteen by forty-eight feet and positioned at prime locations in a market. Both require custom designing and are intended for long-term exposure. Obviously, they are very costly, so you have to evaluate very carefully what your objectives are in choosing this type of outdoor medium. The big advantage, of course, is that they're big and hard to ignore.

INFLATABLES

If you have a reasonably high-visibility location, inflatable displays and mascot costumes can really draw extra attention to your business at a very low cost. The Firestone Mastercare down the street from our office has a three-story-high inflatable tire that it displays three or four times a year. It's obviously shared with other Firestone locations and rotates from store to store. You can't help but see it. The only negative for this tire display is having to make sure it's always inflated. When trying to convey the quality of the company's tires, a huge tire that is going flat and flapping in the wind will not help the cause. The two-story inflatable gorilla touting Samsonite above the luggage store is another example.

An example of a mascot is the Liberty Tax Service mascot (Lady Liberty), which was out by the street waving at cars during tax season. The company's office was in a strip center with no visibility from a very busy street. The mascot drew attention to the location at very little cost. And the cost of that costume is tax deductible.

Very early in my marketing career, I also managed a karate school to make a little extra money. The school was located on one of the busiest streets in the city. To draw extra attention to the school, during the summer I used to hold class outside in the parking lot near the street. As traffic drove by, drivers were drawn to the rows of students dressed in their pajama-like white uniforms and performing punches and kicks in unison while screaming at the top of their lungs with each move. (I got my black belt in marketing long before my one in karate.)

One of my favorite Street Fighter stories is about a business that was running an ad campaign for a special event. To make its location easy to find, the company had a huge inflatable blue balloon for consumers to use as a landmark. That balloon could be seen for miles. The company ran a lot of media about the event, and each spot was tagged, "Look for the big blue balloon." A competitor down the street, on the day of the event, flew his own blue balloon, and it was even bigger. Who do think got the biggest ROMI on that deal?

EMAIL, VOICE MAIL, PHONE, AND FAX

In the new world order of marketing, there are many new buffers to keep your marketing message from reaching the intended targeted potential customer. Email, voice mail, and faxes can all be incorporated into the mix of Street Fighter Marketing Solutions. Voice mail is a major issue for many business people trying to reach their target audience. You have a much better chance of getting someone to return your message if you know some key secrets. Renee Grant-Williams is the voice coach to the stars. Based in Nashville, she tutors such notables as Faith Hill, Tim McGraw, Christina Aguilera, Huey Lewis, and many others. She is the author of *Voice Power: Using Your Voice to Captivate, Persuade, and Command Attention.* The techniques that she uses to get these performers to maximize their star quality on stage and in recordings can also be used by business people to make an impact in voice mail and even in live phone calls.

Renee suggests that a quick, effective message is a great timesaver. She says that your goal in leaving the message should bring you one step closer to the person and the consummation of business together. Leaving the "right" message depends on both content and delivery. The following steps will help you to leave a professional message that increases your chance of getting your call returned:

BE PREPARED

Instead of just seeing voice mail as a chance to leave your name and number, see it as a way to advance your cause. You have one or at the most two opportunities to make a recorded impression. You can't afford to wing it.

CLEARLY STATE YOUR INFORMATION

Following a brief benefit statement, leave your name, company, and telephone number. Say your telephone number clearly, allowing the other person enough time to write it down. Use your full name to identify yourself; it is stronger to say "This is so-and-so" rather than "My name is."

ASK FOR A SPECIFIC ACTION

Rather than just asking someone to call you back, make a specific request. This allows the person to leave you the information you need if you miss the return call.

FOLLOW UP YOUR INITIAL CALL

You can call back without being labeled a pest. Let the person know that you understand how busy he or she is. Saying "If you're not able to get back to me, I'll try to catch you next week" gives the other person an out. Also, if you are leaving several messages, keep notes on what you said during previous calls. You want your messages to sound fresh and spontaneous.

KNOW WHEN TO STOP TALKING

Don't ramble just because you haven't been cut off. Remember, you are taking up someone's time. Your message will be better appreciated if it is brief and to the point.

ADJUST YOUR ATTITUDE

Even though you are talking to a machine, you need to speak to the person. The tone of your voice should reflect the content of your message. If you want to convey an upbeat attitude, smile. It will be heard in your voice.

SCRIPT YOUR MESSAGE

I suggest that you script out your message, because it is too important to leave to chance. Remember, you have only a few seconds before the prospect decides to delete your message, so think of your first sentence as the headline of an ad or the opener to a radio commercial. Grab attention by providing a benefit. Then follow up with your details, like your name, company, and phone number. Repeat your phone number and slow down to give the person time to jot it down.

To illustrate, our Street Fighter outbound message sounds something like this: "Hi, John, I wanted to share with you some of our ideas on the way we teach businesses how to market, promote, and increase sales without spending a lot of money. This is Jeff Slutsky with Street Fighter Marketing. My number is 800-758-8759. That's 800-SLUTSKY. Please give me a call. I'll look forward to taking just a few minutes to share some great information with you. Again, that's 800-758-8759."

Notice that the first sentence is a benefit statement. Create a statement that tells your prospect the end result of having used your product or service.

Usually, I'll leave no more than two voice-mail messages. Anymore than that, and you'll be perceived as a pest. Since one may get deleted prematurely, a second attempt is fine. After the second message, I'll try to find out from the secretary or receptionist when is a good time to catch the prospect in. Sometimes, when requested, a secretary will give you a prospect's email address.

FROM THE MOUTHS OF BABES

If nothing I try works, then I have to get a little creative. That's when I use a simple idea that was taught to me by Orval Ray Wilson, the coauthor of *Guerrilla Teleselling*. I get my son Mitchell on the phone to leave the message for me. He'll say, "Mr. Smith? This is Mitchell Slutsky. My dad, Jeff Slutsky, has been trying to get ahold of you for a while. And he said that he would take me to Disney World just as soon as you return his call." Well, do you think it worked? So far, this year alone, I owe my son fourteen trips to Disney.

AUTO CALLERS

Another way to leave a message is to prerecord it and have a calling machine deliver it to your call list. These machines were originally used by companies to do cold calling by phone. They've been outlawed in most places, and rightfully so, they're very annoying. The recipient answers his phone and gets a prerecorded message. The interested recipient is then able to convey a message on the machine. However, you can use this machine to convey valuable information to a list of customers who have asked to be on your "hot call list" to receive advance notice of sales or special items. As long as each of the numbers on your list has been provided for that purpose with permission, this can be an effective communication tool and a great supplement to email and fax messages.

A COMPETITIVE EXIT STRATEGY HELPS BRING IN OLD CUSTOMERS

When one or more of your competitors goes out of business, dramatically increase your business with a "competitive exit" program. Here are a few tactics that businesses have used successfully:

Get the Old Phone Number

If a competitor has closed its doors in the last several years (and did not sell the business to someone else), consider getting the company's old phone number. To see if that number is available, call it. If you get a recording, your next step is to call your local service provider to see if it can get you that number. Joe Sheneman of Hometown Appliance services pursued such an opportunity and told us that it costs his business less than $30 a month. The old number is simply forwarded to his company's own number. In the first month, he noticed an average increase of 15 percent in his inbound calls. The reason was that the old competitor still had an address and phone sticker out with that phone number; there may have even been a yellow pages ad still being used.

Ask for the Referral

If the old number is currently being used by a noncompetitive business or a person, you can offer to buy the number from that person for a year or so. Pay for the extra phone line, so that the number can be forwarded to your business. If the number holder doesn't want to do that, you might suggest that he will probably be getting calls for your type of business. Tell him that you would appreciate it if he would give your number when he gets those wrong numbers. Then offer to buy him a nice dinner or something for his effort. Sometimes these arrangements can be made directly with the receptionist if the number holder is a business.

If there is a delay because the number has not been released yet, you can do what Bob did for his Cincinnati sewing machine dealership. He called the former owner and offered him $100 to contact the phone company on his behalf to ask for an intercept message. This way, when a customer called the old number, instead of hearing that it had been disconnected, the customer heard that the number had been changed. The new number in the message was Bob's.

Buy the Customer List

A former competitor's mailing list can be a very valuable asset for someone still in the business. Offer to buy the list. Even if the list is a little out of date, it still could provide you with more new customers. Do a series of mailings to that list. Make sure the first mailing is first class so that you can get the returns of the outdated addresses and clean it up for future mailings.

Put Up a Banner

Put up a banner that says "This company is out of business, but if you're looking for someone to take care of your needs, call our number." This was the approach a tire dealer outside of Denver used when his competitor vacated a building across the street. He got permission from the landlord, for a small fee, to put up a banner for a few months with his address, phone number, and the message that he'd honor all the old company's tire warranties.

Mirror Their Advertising

If the competitor has run an ad consistently over the years, run your ad in the same place and at the same times. Make the style of your ad similar to the old competitor's, but with your information.

CLEVER PHONE NUMBERS HELP RING YOUR BELL

Words are worth a thousand phone numbers. Spelling out a key word will make it easier for your customers and prospects to remember your number. For example, advertisements for Able Roofing feature its number, 444-ROOF. Atlas Butler Heating and Cooling ads likewise feature its number: 800-FURNACE. Nationally, companies like 800-FLOWERS and 800-MATTRESS have not only made their numbers memorable, or mnemonic, but also named themselves after their numbers. Another great example is Hooked on Phonics: 800-A-B-C-D-E-F-G. Not to be outdone, we also decided to take advantage of this clever marketing tool by securing 800-SLUTSKY. Nobody else wanted that number, so we grabbed it! Another benefit from using our name in our 800 number is that we also get extra publicity. In most interviews, speakers and authors usually don't get an opportunity to give out their contact information, because it comes off as being too commercial. But in many interviews, I'm usually given a lead-in when interviewers make fun of my last name. When they do, I can launch into a routine about growing up with the last name of Slutsky and end my response by saying, "It's even my 800 number."

When you're looking to get a memorable phone number for your business, here are few tips to help you leverage this valuable marketing tool:

Incorporate Your Phone Number into All of Your Advertising

Include your phone number in all of your advertising, on your letterhead, on vehicles, and everywhere your company name appears. Think of it as an extension of your company name.

Make Sure You Buy Similar Numbers

With all vanity numbers, there can be confusion when converting letters to numbers. If available, secure similar numbers or numbers that are frequently misdialed to reach you. Able Roofing has not only 444-ROOF but also 444-Able and 444-7003. Why the last one? Because sometimes people misread the *O* for a zero. Before Able bought the 7003 number, it was losing around three hundred calls per month. With our number, we reserved it with the last digit as a 4 instead of a 9, because people often spell *Slutsky* as *Slutski*.

Incorporate Your Phone Number into Your URL Address

If you already have a memorable number, turn it into an address on the World Wide Web. This has been done very successfully, for example, with www.800FLOWERS.com.

Spell Out the Number

While a mnemonic number is memorable, callers must still convert the letters to numbers. Make it easy for them. After your word number, place the numerical version in parentheses, italics, or a smaller typeface. We do this in all our promotional pieces: 800-SLUTSKY (*800-758-8759*). However, if your ad or letter asks for an immediate phone call, place the numerical number first, followed by the word number.

Get Creative When Looking for a Memorable Number

For a local number, it's best to use a four-letter word unless the exchange spells out your word perfectly in seven letters. On toll-free numbers, you want to use seven-letter words. Write down several four-letter and seven-letter words that describe your business. Then see if those numbers are available. Perhaps 800-SHINGLE would be a good number for either a roofing company or an infectious disease clinic. Local numbers that spell HEAT or COOL might be great for a heating, ventilating, and air-conditioning company. A number ending in 5325 (LEAK) could be used by a plumber—or a urologist. There are a lot of possibilities.

If Possible, Avoid Words with the Letters *O, I,* or *L*

The letters *O* and *I* can easily be confused with zero and one. The letter *L* can also sometimes be confused with the number one.

EMAIL

Email communications can provide you with an effective way to market to people as long as your message isn't perceived as spam. When sending regular mail doesn't get through, sometimes email can do the job for you. As with regular mail, you must have a credible list. So when you capture a contact's name, mailing address, and phone number, always be sure to ask for the email address, too.

The advantages of email over regular mail are obvious:

1. There's no cost of postage.
2. It's instant.
3. It's interactive and can allow an immediate response.
4. You can send out to as many addresses as you want with one click of the mouse. Consider using email in conjunction with regular mail and other means. Some customers prefer getting your information via email, while others prefer it in other formats. The more options you have, the more likely you are to get your message to the largest number of customers.

In an email, your "subject" line is like the headline in an advertisement. You want to write one that will beckon the recipient to open your email instead of hitting the delete key.

Don't abuse the privilege of contacting a customer by email. Make sure that every time you email someone, you provide real value in the message. Failing to do so will result in your emails being blocked.

The format of your email can take several approaches. It can be as simple as a text message or as elaborate as an e-newsletter complete with photos, graphics, and even animation. The format you choose should depend on your objectives and also your budget.

Since you're relying on the recipient to open your email, it's best used with people who are already aware of you and have expressed an interest in receiving your messages.

E-zine

Renee Grant-Williams uses email to send out a monthly electronic newsletter to approximately three thousand singers, speakers, and related businesses. She calls it the *NewsFlash*. Her *NewsFlash* is created in HTML format with the help of Dream-Weaver web page—design software and delivered via auto-responder software, so that it comes through as a web page, in full color with links, photographs, and animation. Each page of her website (www.MyVoiceCoach.com) has a link with a free token gift to entice people to sign up to receive the *NewsFlash*, which has resulted in a daily increase in the number of recipients. The tangible results are a 107 percent increase of unique visitors to her website since her first issue. This exposure has helped increase sales of her books, and audio and video products through her website by 154 percent.

Signature Line

Make sure to put all of your contact information in your automatic signature line to appear at the bottom of all your emails. Always make it easy for people to get back in touch with you by whatever means is most convenient for them. If possible, include your company logo as well. However, be careful with graphics, because they could slow down the process or even get flagged as spam. When sending a generic email to a number of people in your address book, use the blind-copy function (bcc) so that the email addresses are not shared without permission.

JUST THE FAX

The fax machine can be a powerful alternative or supplement to using email and voice mail. One of the most successful uses of the fax machine I've tried was suggested to me by Hal Becker, author of *Can I Have 5 Minutes of Your Time?* When I have a prospect who's expressed serious interest in our services but has stopped returning my efforts to contact him, I send him a fax that reads:

Dear _____:

I've had a difficult time getting in touch with you to get your feedback about bringing me in to keynote at your annual convention. Please choose one of the options below and fax it back to me right away so I know where we stand.

Please check one and fax back form:

_____ I am ready to do the paperwork now.

_____ I'm still hashing things out. I'm busy now, so please contact me on: [please give a convenient date and time]

_____.

_____ I'm not interested. Please don't call again. Remove my name from your list.

I've gotten about a 50 percent response rate from this fax. Of the responses, they are almost equally divided between the three options.

Broadcast Fax

Unsolicited broadcast faxes are annoying. They are effective when the recipients have opted to receive your fax. I used that method successfully by faxing a monthly article to our clients and prospects. Marc and I were writing a weekly syndicated column for Knight Ridder anyway, so it was easy to change the format to a fax sheet. At the same time that the article was sent to Knight Ridder/Tribune News Service, it was sent to a list of people who wanted to receive an advance copy. It was a great way to stay in touch with these people inexpensively. And since we were already doing the article, it didn't take much time. We also emailed the same article to contacts on our email list. Recipients would choose which way they preferred to receive the weekly article.

You can use the same approach to give your preferred customers advance notice of special offerings. But always give them
the option to be removed from any of your lists.

COMBINATIONS

Prospects are all different, and they respond uniquely to all forms
of communications. Communicating by telephone and by voice
mail may work better for some, while fax or email may work
better for others. In the long run, however, you may want to use
a combination of all of these methods to make the strongest
impact. Add a few clever postcard mailings, and you can develop
a campaign that will allow you to determine which combinations provide the best return on your investment.

PUBLICITY PLAIN AND SIMPLE

Getting local publicity is part of your Street Fighter Marketing Solution. It can make more of an impact than advertising because it's *not* advertising. Your story becomes part of the entertainment, which is the reason people read the publication, listen to the radio station, or watch the TV show. One downside of publicity, however, is that you have to go after it aggressively. Unlike advertising, you can't simply write a check, and you're on the air or in print. You have to sell the media on the newsworthiness of your story. Reporters are not interested in giving you free exposure. However, they are interested in stories that would be of interest or value to their audience.

The other downside is that you have no control over the content of the news item that is being printed or produced about you. There's always the possibility that getting publicity could backfire if the reporter sees something that is not positive about your business.

But given those negatives, the advantages are powerful. More local businesses should look at local publicity as just one more piece of the puzzle, though you can't rely on it to fully promote your business. But it can give your overall marketing program a nice boost from time to time.

One of the first things you need to do is decide if you're going to do the publicity yourself or hire a PR firm. A good local PR firm will likely have some good contacts in the local media. It will likely be able to place stories more easily than you could yourself. For this service, the agency will charge a fee. This fee could be either a monthly retainer or a per-placement charge. Regardless of how the firm charges, you need to evaluate the return on your investment not by how much free press you get but, rather, by how much business the free press creates for you.

PR firms like to have you evaluate them based on the value of the placement compared to that of regular advertising. If you get an article in your local daily newspaper that covers one-third of a page, they evaluate it as if you had purchased a one-third-page ad. From that perspective, it's very fair because, in most cases, an article of equal size should have significantly more impact than the ad.

However, what you really need to do is track your results like you should for any marketing program. Then take the amount of business or profit you generated as a result of all the exposure the PR firm created and subtract out its fee and any other related expenses to arrive at a return on your marketing investment. Just because you get a full-page article or a three-minute feature on the early and late news doesn't mean that the exposure has paid for itself.

For most local businesses, it should be relatively easy to work a simple publicity program into their operations. As in other local marketing efforts, if you spend a little time up front to create a marketing infrastructure, you'll be prepared when the opportunity arises for you to inform the media of a possible news item.

Your first step should be to identify all the publicity outlets in your marketplace that are most appropriate for your business. The reality is that without this advance work, you might not get adequate time to suggest the story, and you'll lose an opportunity for good free publicity.

In addition to the news outlets, you want the names of the reporters or contacts for the various departments or specialties. For all of these contacts, you want their mailing addresses and, if possible, their direct phone lines and personal email addresses. It would also help if you knew how they liked to be contacted (phone, mail, or email).

There are a lot more news outlets than you think. In addition to your major daily newspapers, there are suburban papers, and you probably have several specialty weekly publications geared for business, parents, kids, singles, and religious and ethnic groups, as well as association and organization newsletters, plus several monthly and quarterly magazines. In addition to the major television networks, some cable opportunities probably exist. And with television stations, in addition to their newsrooms, there may be specific programs that could provide you an opportunity. Most radio stations will have newsrooms, but double-check to see if several stations are sharing a news department. Last, look for internet opportunities as well. Nearly every news outlet also has an internet outlet, so even if one doesn't want the story for its traditional news channel, it may use the story on its website. And there may be some website-only opportunities in your marketplace.

With your major daily newspaper, you'll want to have a list of the appropriate editors of the various sections. You have the city desk for the basic news; the business editor; the arts and leisure editor; the religion editor; the home and garden editor; and so on. When you come up with a news story, you should think about which editor would most likely be interested in it. Or you may want to slant your story or create an angle to a specific editor so that you're not inundating one editor all the time. A fund-raising event for a church group at your location, for example, could be slanted to either the business editor or the religion editor. If the group was raising money to revamp the landscape of its church, there might even be a lawn and garden angle as well.

Part of the information you need may already be available in some form. Check to see if there is a PR directory for your marketplace. You can get a lot of this information searching on the web as well. It could also be a nice project for a local college student working on a journalism or PR degree. This list will need to be updated from time to time, since reporters seem to move around a lot.

Next, determine the best way to reach each news contact. Email is becoming the preferred method of contacting most reporters and editors. This makes your job that much easier. If your story idea is very timely and possibly the making of a major feature story, you can even follow up with a phone call.

LEVERAGE PUBLICITY

Once you get some publicity, you want to extend the value of it beyond the original exposure. With permission, you can reprint the items that appeared in print. They can be framed or enlarged to put in your place of business. This allows your existing customers to see what you've done and will hopefully build a little more loyalty. If you get interviewed on the radio, get a recording of it and use it for a while as your "message on hold" on your phone system.

GENERATING PUBLICITY

There are several ways to generate publicity. First, you can report on events that are happening already. A grand opening, a new manager, a title promotion, the introduction of a new product or service, and a charity fund-raiser are all examples of business events that might be of interest to the right reporters. It may not get you a full feature story, but even a mention in another article or a small blurb helps. The other way to generate publicity is to create an event specifically to capture the attention of the news media. For TV interviews, you can have someone take some pictures of you getting interviewed and create a flyer of the event. If the TV picture is good enough, you can even convert some TV images to print as well. You can use excerpts from all the PR in your brochures or other promotional items. For example, we were featured in *Inc.* magazine with the headline "Brains over Bucks." So we use that as a quote along with the *Inc.* name under it in many of our promotional pieces. It's simple and powerful.

But the most dramatic example of how powerful a news story can be came when I was featured in the *Wall Street Journal*. My company was not quite three years old, and I was a one-man shop, struggling for survival. I knew I had something unique to offer to clients, but my Street Fighter concepts were a far different approach to marketing than most business people were used to.

At the time, I had a relationship with S&S Public Relations in Chicago. I had interned for Steve Simon, who taught me a great deal about working with the news media and getting stories placed. S&S would do my PR for me in exchange for me training their newest account executive (AE), who would be assigned my account. In effect, I was the account supervisor for my own business. It was a great arrangement.

We did the normal types of PR stuff. I would help the new AE develop the press release, the press kit, and the list of targets, which would include all the major business publications. Then I would help her learn how to follow up with the various reporters by telephone. This approach got me various interviews on radio stations around the country, as well as features in the *Chicago-Sun Times, Nation's Business,* and a host of trade journals and dailies. Some of the stories would generate a phone call or two but not much in actual sales.

Then I hit the equivalent of the publicity Powerball. The *Wall Street Journal* called. It was a reporter by the name of Frank James, working out of the Chicago bureau. He interviewed me. Then he called back several times to get additional details. He then checked out every story I gave him. It was the most thorough interview I'd ever been through. Finally, Frank called and said the story would run sometime the next week.

I was very excited. I knew that a paragraph or two in the *Wall Street Journal* would definitely bring me some clients. Tuesday night I got a phone call from a guy who had lived on my dorm floor at Indiana University. He said that he worked for the *Wall Street Journal* in Wisconsin, and his job was laying out the pages for the paper. He told me that my story would be in Wednesday's paper on the front page of the second section. It included a sketch of me, and the article started at the top of the page, went down the entire page, one-column wide, and finished deeper in the section.

That was exciting. I couldn't ask for better placement. I knew this article would generate some business. I made a point of setting my alarm to get up at eight in the morning so that I could prepare for the phone calls. At that time, I was working out of my home office. The phone started ringing at *six* o'clock! As soon as I would hang up, the phone would ring again. The calls went on till ten o'clock that night. Most of the calls were sales of my audio album, and some were inquiries about seminars and speeches. The same thing happened the next day. Each successive day there were fewer calls, but those calls came in solid for three months. Even after that, I got a call at least once a week for up to a year afterward. That one lead turned into a six-figure consulting contract.

You would be lucky to get this type of PR once in a lifetime, but if you don't have a regular PR effort as part of your Street Fighter Marketing Solution, you'll never have the opportunity.

HANDLING A PR CRISIS

We were promoting one of our seminars. We had the support of the local chamber of commerce in that city and provided a special "member to member" discount to the chamber members. To help market the event to its members, the chamber provided us an email list of nearly two thousand addresses and permission to send our message to them. What started out as an economical marketing program turned into a marketing nightmare.

We first noticed a problem that evening when we started getting "mailer daemons" every few seconds. Within an hour, there were over five hundred emails to our address. Apparently there was a virus; a hacker caused our email to be replicated repeatedly to everyone on the list. Not only was our email account getting overloaded, so were those of the two thousand people on that list. Each one of them thought they were getting hundreds of emails from us. There were some angry people, to say the least.

This is a classic marketing crisis. The problem was totally out of our control, yet we were getting a lot of negative PR. So we immediately went into crisis mode, taking the following steps:

1. Identify the problem. In our case, the problem was an email message that masqueraded as if it had come from us, and it was transmitted literally hundreds of times to each individual email box.
2. Develop a response. We started getting phone calls. Since the email originally went out on a Friday night, we actually got calls at our home on Saturday. In a line of defense, we had to

script what we would say: First, we told them that we were aware of the problem. Second, we apologized for the inconvenience, noting that it was just as big an inconvenience for us as for them. Third, we asked that they please understand that these emails were not coming from us. Fourth, we told them that we were doing everything we could to solve the problem.

We made sure that everyone on the phones followed that format. Plus, no matter the tone of the caller, the people manning our phones were to be pleasant and apologetic. Of the many dozens of calls we received, the vast majority of people understood and were empathetic once we explained the situation. We also changed the outbound message of our voice mail to explain the problem. Once the inbound calls slowed down to a trickle, we changed the outbound message back to the original message.

3. Fix the problem, if it's fixable. We called AOL, which started an investigation for us. We also contacted our information technology provider to see if it could figure out anything. Next, we contacted the chamber. It too had received many phone calls. We explained the situation, and like everyone else, the chamber's administration was very understanding. We offered to write a brief article explaining the situation in the chamber's weekly newsletter.

4. Make sure it never happens again.

DATA MINING, INTELLIGENCE GATHERING, AND COVERT OPERATIONS
(Street Fighter Special Forces)

Your database of customers is perhaps the most valuable asset you have in your business. It is literally a diamond in the rough just waiting for you to discover those few precious marketing jewels within its bytes. A key Street Fighter Solution is to not only mine for those rough nuggets of high value but learn how to refine your efforts into a marketing equivalent of a flawless, brilliant center stone. Now, while data mining is used to predict trends, the Street Fighter approach uses data mining to create sales.

Through the use of automated statistical analysis (or data mining) techniques, businesses are discovering new trends and patterns of behavior that previously went unnoticed. Once they've uncovered this vital intelligence, it can be used in a predictive manner for a variety of applications.

In its very basic form, data mining can be as simple as the business card drawing mentioned in chapter 5. That simple approach allows you to capture a large number of clients' valuable information. And, of course, it's most applicable in a retail setting, where you have a large customer base and generally don't get an opportunity to know your customers on a first-name basis.

> When you uncover more information about your customers, more opportunities rise to the surface.

On the complete opposite end of the spectrum is the type of database created by Target America, a company that provides very specialized data for nonprofit organizations and financial companies. According to Jim McGee, the CEO and founder:

Target America's database, culled from seventy-five data sources, contains more than seven million records of the wealthiest and most generous people in the nation—the top 5 percent in terms of income, assets, and philanthropic history. Ninety-four percent of the individuals on the database give more than $5,000 a year to charities. The breadth of our data is unique: We focus not only on high-profile corporate America, but include emerging sources of wealth such as minority-owned business and women entrepreneurs.

Nancy Johnson, the president and COO, explained how the information could be useful. Consider a nonprofit agency that gets donations from a number of people each year. On this list is a certain donor who religiously donates $25 each year when she is called during the annual fund drive. What this agency does not know is that this woman donates about *$25,000* a year to various causes. By running its list of donors through the Target America database, it's possible to identify which donors (regardless of donation size) are actually in the top 5 percent of the wealthiest people in the United States. Armed with that piece of information, an organization might want to consider a more comprehensive marketing approach, which could be something as simple as inviting her to lunch, having the chairperson make a personal phone call, or some other strategy that could potentially build a stronger relationship with this prospect who could be a tremendous asset to the organization.

This information also tells the organization that this donor sits on the boards of a couple of public companies with other like-minded women. Each of them donates between $50,000 and $175,000 a year to various causes, though not to this organization. If it knew that piece of valuable information, it could then use some of the Street Fighter Marketing tactics to perhaps convince her and her friends to become donors. (To test Target America's program for free, log on to www.tgtam.com/freetest.php.)

The Target America program was initially developed for nonprofits, political fund-raising, and health care fund-raising. However, it has expanded into financial services. This type of approach can be tremendously powerful for anyone selling investments, insurance, real estate, and other products or services that are commonly purchased by the top 5 percent of the wealthiest people. This makes perfect sense. You may have a client that has an investment account with your company. What you don't know is that your client may have several other accounts with other companies, including retirement accounts, college savings accounts, and so on. It should be a lot easier to get an existing client to consolidate all of his or her accounts with you than to generate the same amount of new business by cold-calling. But this type of data mining goes much further. Not only can you identify if an exiting customer is in the top 5 percent, but you can determine all of his or her key business relationships. Perhaps this customer sits on the board of several companies or foundations.

You then find out the names of the other board members. It's no longer cold calling. You have a point of reference, and if you service your customers properly, many should be willing to give you an introduction.

This type of data mining is what is currently available. You can use a service like Target America, or you may be able to find out some of this information on your own. The Street Fighter Solution is based on this type of approach growing way beyond the nonprofits and financial services in the future.

Think about any type of high-end product or service where this approach would be applicable: Mercedes or Lexus dealerships, upscale jewelry stores, fine-art galleries, agencies providing luxury homes for sale or lease, specialty fashion boutiques, furriers, yacht brokers, luxury cruise and specialty travel providers, time-share marketers, agents for resort homes, home-theater providers, security system providers, and so forth. Plus, this approach doesn't have be limited to just the wealthiest consumers. If your target audience happens to be between the top 10 percent and 20 percent, you could follow the same procedures to make the information work for you.

The downside of this approach, of course, is the amount of time it takes to develop the database. However, there will soon be a variety of providers that will be developing databases like this for just about any group. The key is to use the information once you get it so that you can generate a healthy return on your investment.

The more focused your target list is, the more efficient you can be in contacting the people on the list. Mass mailing is tremendously inefficient, which is why 98 percent of it is tossed out. But with a stronger list, fully researched and indexed, you can afford to create messages more specific to the reader. You also can afford to send more elaborate pieces that would be cost prohibitive in a mass-mail setting.

THE MOST PROFITABLE

One exercise we have clients do is to identify which segment of their customer base brings them the most profit. This doesn't necessarily mean the highest-volume buyers. And when we look at profitability, we look at more than margin. We also look at how much of your internal resources are needed to properly service that account. You may have an account that provides you good volume and decent margins but takes up so much of your time in keeping the customer happy that it may not be as profitable as you thought.

The purpose of the exercise, of course, is to try identifying those client traits you would most like to replicate when looking for future clients. Instead of seeking any and all newcomers to your business, you can focus your marketing and sales efforts on a narrow target audience that will provide you the best overall return on your investment—not just in relation to marketing costs but in relation to the cost of maintaining that client.

> Identify the traits in a customer you would most like to replicate.

Once you quantify those desirable characteristics, use your Street Fighter data mining tactics to root out leads that will closely emulate that segment of your customer base. For example, when we are prospecting for clients to sell a major neighborhood marketing sales project, we look to our previous clients as a guide. The first piece of the matrix is the business model: chains, franchises, and independents. Then, there's the number of units in the marketplace. Next we look at growth in both same-store sales and new units. The type of client most likely to invest the necessary funds to develop and implement such a large project is a business that has both franchises and company-owned units where one or the other is at least 25 percent of the total.

If a company is showing a lot of growth in sales and is expanding a lot, it probably won't be willing to commit the resources, both financial and internal, to make comprehensive neighborhood marketing work for it. It's easier just to throw a bunch of money against the mass media to drive sales, regardless of its ROMI. But when things slow down, and franchisees complain that corporate isn't doing enough, then its mass media advertising budget is maxed out, and it needs to do something dramatic to jump-start the organization. The company has to have a minimum of fifty units to consider such a project, and there needs to be a lack of market penetration with most of them. That is, such a project is an option when not enough units located exist in a single ADI ("area of dominant influence" used by Arbitron) or DMA to consider the use of mass media in that market. Assuming the operational part of the business is still strong, we know we can make a big impact for the business and, more important, that the client is more likely to take our advice and not water down the program. That's not to say that other combinations within that matrix wouldn't be effective. It's just that we know that this ideal matrix is easier to sell and more easily provides a strong ROMI on our work.

The point is, instead of taking any business that happens to contact you, create a very specialized hit list and get creative and aggressive in going after the people on it. In the meantime, if some low-hanging fruit happens to find its way to you, pluck it.

Data Capture

The key to any successful data mining program is the capture of the information from the customer. This capture needs to be done in a nonintrusive way, so as to not offend your customer. Again, the business card drawing is one nonintrusive example. If you want to capture information about your customers' home environments, you can still run a fishbowl drawing, but instead of using their business cards, have your customers fill in entry forms. With an entry form, you can capture the specific information you want.

Keep in mind that if you request too much detail on an entry form, your customers may not want to participate in your drawing. To help you in this area, consider the "long form" entry for your contest, which involves your presenting the possibility of winning a prize in your drawing. The entry form asks for the basic information: name, home address, phone, email, and, perhaps, age, birthday, place of work, or several other items. Then, on the form and also on the poster, let the participant know that he can double the prize by filling out the additional ten questions on the form. It's an option. The additional questions would provide you with some key information that you are trying to capture.

You may get a number of inbound calls inquiring about your services, but callers may be hesitant about giving you information. Caller ID, if not blocked, gives you enough information to get started. With a phone number, you can track down a mailing address and market directly to the caller without that person realizing he has been targeted.

You do want to temper your desire to capture your customers' contact information with their willingness to give it. Your first priority should be to provide a positive buying experience. Then you can capture the information, provided that it doesn't interfere with developing good customer relations.

My absolute favorite example of data capture gone wrong is told by my good friend Larry Winget, one of the most gifted personal development speakers and author of *It's Called* Work *for a Reason!* He shares this story:

I was walking through the mall one day when I realized I needed to stop and buy some batteries. I saw a store in the mall I knew sold batteries, so I headed toward it. I pulled the batteries off the rack and laid the batteries on the counter along with my cash. A guy on the other side of the counter looked at me and said, "Can I have your name, address, and telephone number?" Have you ever had that happen? Of course you have. I said, "No." Want to start having some fun in life? Then just get good at saying no. Stores don't have any idea what to do when the customer just real politely says no.

So the guy at the counter said to me, "Sir, we have to have your name, address, and telephone number in order to sell you the batteries." I asked him why. He then went on to tell me the number-one thing that no customer ever wants to hear. He said, "Sir, because that is our company policy." I told him I had a "customer policy," and that my customer policy was that for $1.79 worth of batteries, when I was paying cash, I didn't need to tell him who I was.

At that point, he pushed the batteries across the counter and said he wouldn't be able to sell me the batteries. I asked if there was a manager there. He told me the manager was in the back but he would go get him. He then went in the back and came out with what I recognized right off to be a manager: It was a kid about nineteen years old. You've seen this guy, haven't you?

The manager approached the counter with his finger pointed at me, stopped in front of me with that finger about a foot from my nose and said, "Sir, do you have a problem?"

I told him I didn't have any problem at all. He had batteries, and I had money, and in America we call that . . . a deal. He said, "You are going to have to give us your name, address, and telephone number, or we are not going to sell you the batteries." I explained it just wasn't going to happen. I knew he had a company policy, but I had a customer policy. Besides, I told him, I wanted him, as the manager, to explain to me why it was necessary to give all of my personal information when I was paying cash. He then told me the second thing no customer ever wants to hear: "Because that's the way we've always done it."

I told him I had really good news for him, because on that day, he was going to get to find a way to do it differently.

At that point, he pushed the batteries across the counter at me and said, "We aren't doing business with you!" and turned to walk away. I said, "Listen, you are the manager, and I am the customer. You should be able to figure out some way for me to get the product that I came in here for and, believe it or not, am still willing to pay for, so don't walk away until you at least stop and think about this for a minute."

He stopped, thought for a while, turned, and walked over to his computer, where he started to type. In just a minute, he took my money and handed me some change. Then he put the batteries in a bag along with a receipt that he pulled from his computer, saying to me, "There you go, I figured it out."

I asked him what he had figured out. He told me that he had just put his own name, address, and telephone number on my receipt.[19]

DATA MINING YOUR COMPETITION

Next to your own customer database, the most valuable database you can get is that of your competitor. A pizza restaurant used to drive to the competition's location and write down the license plate numbers of the cars in its lot. Those numbers were converted to names and mailing addresses. The list was compared against the pizza restaurant's own customer database. If there was a name that showed up on both databases, that person received a moderate discount in the mail. If the name did not show up on the database, that person received a big discount to motivate him to go to the restaurant for a first-time trial. The danger of this approach, of course, is that if your customers find out what you're doing, it could create ill will in the community. For that reason, we don't usually recommend it.

Another approach we don't recommend—but which can be successful nonetheless—was done by a jewelry store with the help of the owner's friend, who owned a health club. You've no doubt seen the boxes on countertops in different retail establishments that offer free health club memberships. The customer of that restaurant or video rental place fills out the form and puts it in the box. The jewelry store owner had his buddy put those boxes in several of the competing jewelry stores around town. The prize to be drawn was a $50 gift certificate from the store that was permitting the box drawing. What the store owners didn't know was that after the drawing was made, the health club owner gave the entry forms to his friend who owned the jewelry store. He now has a list of his competitors' customers.

FOLLOW THE LEADER

Sometimes good business intelligence simply takes initiative. Consider the owner of a Kansas-based company that sold water treatment systems for homes. When his salespeople complained that they didn't have any good leads, he spent the better part of the day in an affluent neighborhood following the Culligan delivery truck around and writing down the addresses of each delivery. Using a crisscross directory, he generated fifty leads, people who were already spending about $30 a month on filtered water. He explained to his salespeople that their product would pay for itself in short order, and the leads were out there if they were willing to work to capture the information.

One of my all-time favorite examples of data mining before Al Gore invented the internet was used by Chuckles the Clown in Fort Wayne, Indiana. He would visit the "morgue" at the local daily newspaper and look at the birth announcements from five years earlier. His target audience was the parents of five-year-olds who might hire him for their children's birthday parties. With the names in hand, we would develop a database with addresses and phone numbers from which he would market. Of course, the internet makes that type of activity easier to do now, but the idea is the same.

A similar approach can be used to create a list of "divorces granted" from vital statistics in local newspapers. Three months later, the people on that list would probably pay attention to advertisements for a dating service, teeth whitening products, and weight loss programs. If you sell items that would make a great anniversary gift, you could look at wedding announcements. Focus on marketing to husbands, and be sure to cross-reference any anniversary dates you have with divorces filed or granted, to make sure the married couples are still together.

EXPANDING YOUR HORIZONS WITH EVENTS

Events can be a powerful way of breaking through the clutter and making real headway with the return on your marketing investment. Unlike many of the Street Fighter Marketing Solutions presented so far, however, events generally take a lot more time and money. For that reason, it is critical that you examine the purpose of organizing your event and what you expect to achieve with respect to tangible results.

THE BLOWOUT PROMOTION

Sometimes it is just cheaper and more effective to simply give it away than sell it at a discount through traditional advertising. That's the idea behind the "blowout" promotion. Its purpose is to generate an enormous amount of first-time users to try your product or service in a very short time. It has to be executed just right, or it can backfire on you. So be careful! But done properly, it is a perfect way of putting a business on the map or rejuvenating sales.

Consider Luby's Cafeteria in Tampa. Its management planned a customer appreciation day for its blowout promotion. The offer was outrageous: half off everything for one day. To add to the festivities, a banjo player, a magician, and a balloon artist kept the guests entertained while they waited to be seated. The interior of the restaurant was decorated to reinforce the festive spirit. To be successful, there had to be enough food to support the promotion. If the restaurant ran out of product halfway through such a promotion, the results would be disastrous, and the event would end up doing just the opposite of what was planned.

The power of this type of promotion is in getting many first-timers to try your business. Since the prices offered are so ridiculously low, it's clear to everyone that this is a onetime special event. Therefore, you don't risk eroding your regular-price credibility as you could with the overuse of coupons and sales. In this event, the management knew from experience to expect the guests to try the most expensive meals, so they stocked up on fish and meats. This was no time to get cheap. Let them sample your best wares, because when they return, you're more likely to get them to buy your more profitable items.

Not only do you need to have enough product, but you also need to make sure that you have enough labor. Luby's decided this promotion was so important that it had all the other Luby's general managers in the area lend a helping hand. (It also exposed the other managers to the possibilities of similar events at their locations.) Using management proved to be a great asset, because when the cafeteria was packed, and everybody was under a great deal of pressure to perform, they had experienced staff.

> During the event, sales *tripled* and customer counts *quadrupled*. Sales for the month went up.

Sales tripled for the day, and customer counts quadrupled. The important factor here is that sales were up 13 percent for the month following the promotion. The manager estimated that half the people coming to this event were new. To generate the same net results through traditional advertising would have cost significantly more even when getting a higher margin.

It's critical to offer a bounce-back certificate. This is really the only way you'll be able to track how many of the participants in the blowout came back again. Also, it provides all those new customers an opportunity to get a great value on their next visit. The bounce-back offers those new customers an incentive to return to your operation under more normal circumstances. In so doing, you have a much better chance of building a good regular customer. The bounce-back is one of those often forgotten elements of successful promotions. It's a little piece of paper that provides a modest savings or value added when a customer returns. The most important purpose of this bounce-back certificate is twofold: (1) to provide monetary incentive to redeem it; and (2) to track how many people returned after attending your event.

Remember, the purpose of the blowout is not to give stuff away. It's to motivate new customers to visit you for the first time and experience your business at its best. You'll find that it doesn't take a lot of advertising exposure to get the word out on this promotion, since the offer itself is so strong. Sometimes local radio stations will want to jump on the bandwagon and make their own promotions, and you'll end up getting free advertising as well. But don't start advertising internally to your own customers until about four or five days out. Expect the days leading up to the promotion to be slower than usual.

This type of promotion works best when done perhaps once a year. And it should never be done more than twice a year. If you have multiple locations in the marketplace, do only one location at a time.

Pick a good day of the week, but not your best. For a restaurant, video rental store, car wash, and so on, you would *not* want to run such a promotion on a Friday or Saturday. At the same time, if Mondays and Tuesdays are normally dead, you should probably plan on a Thursday promotion.

Think when it makes sense to run such a promotion. One time is just ahead of the grand opening of a new competitor. Another time is leading or trailing a big season. The offer is critical too. Depending on your type of operation, drop the price on your most popular mainstream items. A fast-food place can offer 25¢ hamburgers or tacos for a dime, but not both. Charge full price for everything else. When gas tops $3 a gallon, 99¢ gas will have them lining up for miles, as would a large pizza with any three toppings for $1.99; 99¢ haircuts; and a massage for a penny or a nickel a minute with a fifteen-minute limit. A coffee house can offer premium coffee drinks for a dime; a car wash can provide full service for a quarter; a quick-oil-change provider can promote a $4.99 service; a photo-processing store can market four-by-six-inch color prints for a penny; a quick-print shop can offer color copies for the price of black and white; a dry cleaner can wash and press dress shirts for a dime; and an office-supply or electronics store can offer one hundred blank CD-Rs or twenty DVDs for a buck and a case of copy paper for the price of a ream. The price has to be crazy low. You lose money on each transaction. Of course, you can place reasonable limits on the amount one person can buy.

Contact your key vendors to let them know what you have in mind. Sometimes they'll donate product, and your rep will come out to help because the vendors know it will create more orders for them in the long run. You'll get word-of-mouth exposure, and it's possible to even get publicity in the local media. But that is just the icing on the cake.

OFF-SITE EVENT

Consumer Shows

The most common off-site event is the consumer show. Sports, vacation, boat, car, health, and home and garden are just a few of the types of shows that are produced in most markets. You pay a premium to participate in these events because the event brings thousands of potential buyers to you. To get a good return from your participation, use the show as a means to collect good leads. Ask an attendee a couple of questions to see if he is remotely in a position to buy and use your product or service. Don't spend too much time with any one person, because in doing so, you will let too many opportunities walk by your booth. Capture those qualified names. Then, after the event, do the follow-up. The follow-up is where you make your money.

Organic Event

This off-site event is even more involved and requires a commitment in money and personnel to pull off properly. To consider such a promotion, you have to have a clear idea of what you expect to accomplish from such an investment. You must decide if planning this kind of event will somehow cut your costs or increase your sales. If not, the effort is not justifiable.

Consider a team of regional pharmaceutical representatives working for Bristol-Myers Squibb. They need to get in front of doctors to present their message, or detail, about their products. At best, a rep will have five minutes of less than quality time to tell the story about the drugs he is selling. To help them get more quality time with doctors, we offered a Street Fighter Solution. This team of reps was able to get about one hundred doctors and their spouses to a night of dining and entertainment. So far, this is not a new idea. Their goal was to present information about four different drugs used in the treatment of diseases, including hypertension and diabetes. The show started out with LaDonna Gatlin (baby sister of famed country stars the Gatlin Brothers), who did about thirty minutes of her regular stage performance. She was followed by the comedian and professional speaker Steve Rizzo, with thirty minutes of his clean stuff.

Where the Street Fighter Solution came in was with the grand finale. In order for these events to be justified, there has to be a certain amount of medical information presented. Usually they have a guest speaker presenting this information, and, more times than not, it's pretty dry.

But this group did it differently. Instead of the boring technical presentation, the same information was presented in a twenty-minute musical program that I had written and which was performed by LaDonna and Steve. Using the original music from one of the most beloved musicals of all time, *The Sound of Music,* I wrote eight songs that presented information about those drugs. I wrote the lyrics based on all the technical indications for the drugs. The lyrics were so accurate that the legal department thought they were written by a doctor! Some of the songs included such lyrics as: "The halls are alive with the sounds of mucus," to the tune of "The Sound of Music"; "Claim every patient," to the tune of "Climb Ev'ry Mountain"; "What do you got to help with diarrhea," to the tune of "How do you solve a problem like Maria?"; "There is a chart of a man with a goiter," to the tune of "The Lonely Goatherd"; and, my favorite, about a high-blood-pressure pill that went, "You're 216 over 117," to the tune of "Sixteen Going on Seventeen." LaDonna and Steve received two standing ovations.

Consider that there were one hundred doctors receiving twenty uninterrupted minutes of details about four drugs, delivered in a way so that they wanted to hear more. This was not a cheap event, but from a ROMI standpoint, it worked. The cost of the entire evening was a fraction of what it costs to make this same kind of impact in the field. Granted, it does take a special kind of talent to create such an event, but in the twenty-first century, this kind of impact will be critical. Plus, the doctors were more receptive to meet with those reps after this event.

To put on a program like this is a lot more involved than it may first appear. And it's way too easy for such an effort to end up appearing like a weak amateur production. To really generate a return on your investment, you must create a topnotch event that addresses specific high-value issues. Here are some tips:

A parody works best. I've seen attempts with original music, and they never work. The music is unfamiliar and usually not very good. Corporate musicals composed and written by Ian Seeberg are the exception.[20] According to an article in the *Wall Street Journal,* Mr. Seeburg has written some twenty musicals for clients like Waste Management, Sun Microsystems, Bank of America, Redken, and Wal-Mart. In his shows, he uses key phrases, key acronyms, and jokes that only people inside the company would get.

With a parody, on the other hand, you get to use the most popular tunes ever created. Parody has been a very popular format for the Capitol Steps, who sing political songs, and also for Forbidden Broadway, who poke fun at current musicals in New York. Both troupes have been performing for years and have a strong following. Then there are performers like Weird Al Yankovic, who does many hilarious parodies. Since their subject matter is just for fun, bringing in these performers would not accomplish what you want. You have to create your own show.

First, the original script is of key importance. This is the first weak link. A weak script dilutes the power of this type of an event as a marketing tool. We've found that a parody makes the biggest impact when done right—when you can present your information in a framework that is familiar to the audience. Use a professional writer, because amateur writers will not make it work right for you. By changing the lyrics of well-known songs, there's a point of reference that can make for really good humor. However, there is a real art to matching the content with the right song, using just the right lyrics, and figuring out the right performers to present it.

The issue of legality is generally brought up when dealing with parody. Repeatedly, parody has been a protected form of communication by the courts. The most recent case was *Acuff-Rose v. 2 Live Crew* over the song "Oh Pretty Woman." In 1996 a case was brought before the Supreme Court because the rap group 2 Live Crew used, without permission, "Oh Pretty Woman," originally recorded and cowritten by Roy Orbison. Of course, the X-rated rap group's version was very different from the original. The bottom line is that the Court feels that under most circumstances, parody should be a protected form of speech as long as it doesn't hurt the original owner, the work is changed significantly, and the work fosters discussion. It can even be a work for profit, as long as the other three conditions are met.

From what I've been told, using a parody to educate your audience about your products, services, procedures, and so forth meets those conditions. Keep in mind that anybody can sue anybody over anything. But if you take your case to the Supreme Court, you probably stand a good chance of winning.

Just because a parody is legal doesn't necessarily make it funny or persuasive. Most of these types of productions fall far short. Get a really good writer. One of the vital elements of a song parody is how well the new words fit the original song. There needs to be some kind of reference to the original song lyrics that the audience identifies with, but then the audience should be taken for a sharp left turn. For example, when LaDonna Gatlin opened the grand finale of the show by singing in her best Julie Andrews–type voice, "The halls are alive with the sounds of mucus . . ." it got a big laugh. Everyone knew the music, and the beginning part of the lyric is close to the original. Then the last word of the phrase, *mucus,* took the audience by surprise. Keep in mind that the audience was made up of doctors, so the imagery made sense from their perspective. If the group was made up of Subway franchisees, that line obviously wouldn't work.

Even though parody is protected against copyright infringement, actual performances are not. That means if you want to use music soundtracks, you have to buy the right to do so. Or you can hire your own musicians to create custom soundtracks. For the doctors, LaDonna's husband, Tim, produced all the background music himself in the studio for us. I've also used a live keyboard player for other shows; that worked extremely well.

Another technique is to match the music to the message. Some shows are full parodies of entire musicals like *The Sound of Music, Grease,* and *The Wizard of Oz.* Others can be a collection of songs with some common theme, such as "the best of Broadway" or "oldies." The important point is that the audience must be very familiar with each song you choose to parody. If they don't know the music or the original lyrics, your version won't make that much sense.

In one show we did for the National Speakers Association, one of the big topics was "fee credibility" and how to make sure there is integrity in the pricing for professional speakers. That issue was addressed with Olivia Newton-John's song "Hopelessly Devoted to You." In our version, Jane Jenkins Herlong, a former Miss South Carolina, sings "Helplessly Devalued for You." There were enough triggers in my version to tie it to the original. The closer you get in sound and meter, the funnier it is.

When I'm writing a show like this, I first come up with one song that helps me set the tone for the rest of the show. To start that process, I write down a list of every word or phrase, especially technical jargon, from that industry or company. These are terms that the audience would use every day but are probably not used outside of that environment. These terms draw in the audience because they know this is about them. Most entertainment at conventions is about the entertainer. The parody show, on the other hand, is totally about the issues, problems, people, and opportunities of the audience.

The songs you choose are equally as important. You want songs that focus on the lyrics. Your lyrics are your message. This is where you get your return on investment. Ballads work the best, but you can't sing one ballad after another. So upbeat songs are mixed in. The lyric has to be so simple that the audience can follow it. We also suggest trying to slow down the pace of the song to make it easier for the audience to hear the lyrics. Also, it is a good idea to provide a copy of the lyrics in a program so that the audience members can follow along.

THE BIG EVENT

The most involved event you'll do for your franchisees, dealers, managers, or resellers is your annual convention. This is a huge investment in money and other resources. As mentioned before, once a year, a company will bring in its frontline people. That could be its franchisees, store managers, dealers, and agents, along with vendors and the corporate support people. It is an opportunity to introduce new ideas, procedures, products, and services. It also is used to fire up the troops and help different groups network. When introducing and maintaining a Street Fighter Marketing program throughout your company, the annual convention is where it generally gets kicked off. With the massive cost of one of these events, it is critical that companies and organizations demand a much higher return on their investment. Here are ways to avoid some key money wasters:

There are hundreds of tremendous keynote speakers that are not household names. Fees can range from $5,000 to $25,000, and they can speak about a variety of subjects that are more in line with your goals for your convention. A professional keynoter can present information in a way that will get your attendees to remember it. They have varied styles, so you should be able to find a speaker whose style makes the most sense for your event. And although the speaker might not be a household name before the event, he or she certainly will be to your group after giving the keynote. Most speakers have published books. Negotiate an arrangement where every attendee gets a copy of the book at a good price. Have your keynoter autograph the books afterward. The cost of a professional keynoter and the books would still be far less then a minimal-content celebrity speaker.

Many keynoters will be available to conduct additional breakout sessions for a very nominal add-on fee. Normally you would not be able to get this kind of talent for a breakout for that little money, but you can when you find a keynoter who can perform double duty for you. A professional keynoter often is a lot more willing to provide added value where a celebrity won't. Ask for articles the keynoter has written, for reprinting in your newsletter or on your website. For a small fee, many will allow you to record their session in audio and/or video so that you can send it to people who couldn't make the convention.

Your task is to find that perfect keynoter who will do everything you want to get done so that you can maximize your return on your investment—not just the honorarium for the speaker but the entire cost of the convention. With so much money being invested, every session needs to support your payback goals.

Boring Industry Speakers

On the other end of the spectrum are the free industry speakers. They know their material, but they put their audiences to sleep. For a modest investment in a professional speaker, you can get someone who will adapt your information into a presentation that will make an impact with the audience. What good is presenting the information if your audience won't remember it ten minutes after the presentation is over?

The common thread here is that every detail of your convention or meeting needs to be planned so that it helps you address key issues. Each presenter, entertainer, and giveaway is carefully selected based on its ability to show you that return on your investment in the event. Turn that convention into a powerful tool, but in a way that the audience feels that it got the same amount of entertainment as before. That's where the future needs to be.

What I am suggesting is a more elaborate production than the one described earlier that would more or less be in skit format. This production would be a full-blown forty-five-minute Broadway-style musical produced specifically about your issues and opportunities. Obviously, this is an expensive undertaking, but it is significantly less costly than the big names that corporations often bring in to wow their attendees. For less money, you can deliver a show that entertains on a high level, while teaching, informing, and reinforcing your key corporate messages. This is not an easy task, but when done right, it's perhaps the ultimate Street Fighter Solution.

THE WIZARD OF SALES

With the success of the Bristol-Myers Squibb *Sound of Mucus* show and the National Speakers Association version of *Grease*, it became obvious to Steve Rizzo and me that we were on to something. Steve calls me one day and asks me to write him a one-man show that he can do in addition to his standard keynote speech. Since Steve is a gifted impressionist, the parodies could involve using his unique talents.

Both of us speak to a lot of sales organizations, so we agreed that the show should be geared to salespeople, but it should be general enough that the basic framework could be recycled. With a rewrite, we wanted to be able to adapt it to the unique needs and issues of a given client. It would be a custom show, but many of the most expensive elements of the show would be reusable to help make it cost effective for everyone.

I called Steve back two weeks later with good news and bad news. The good news was that I had already completed a rough draft of his one-man show. The bad news was that it took a cast and crew of twelve to perform it. That's when I suggested we do a parody of the *The Wizard of Oz* for salespeople. First of all, every person knows all the music intimately, as well as all the characters and the plot. For our pilot version, the four main characters would have to overcome four basic selling issues that nearly everyone in a sales audience would identify with. Dorothy would have problems closing the sale. The Scarecrow wouldn't be able to generate good qualified leads. The Tin Man would have a problem handling objections. And the Cowardly Lion (played brilliantly by Steve Rizzo) would have telephone-call reluctance.

The way it's written, the production is both a parody and sequel of sorts. Dorothy, after graduating from Kansas State University, gets a job as a sales rep. In her office are three other salespeople: Hunk, Hickory, and Zeke (also played by Steve Rizzo). The sales manager is Mr. Marvel. And her big competitor, who keeps stealing away her best sales, is Elmira Gulch.

After losing yet another sale to Elmira (this time because of price), she sings, "Somewhere over my sales goals . . ." Throughout the production, each character learns to overcome his or her particular sales issue.

To ensure that the production was of the highest quality, Broadway director Michael Leeds staged and choreographed the entire production with the help of Broadway musical director Phil Reno. The costumes were designed by Tony Award winner Alvin Colt, who also did the costumes for Forbidden Broadway. His concept was to give each character the "business version" of its movie counterpart. Dorothy wears a blue gingham business dress. Hickory is in a stylish silver gray business suit that later turns into his tin business suit. Huck wears a sport coat and tie but is transformed into the Scarecrow, stuffed with shredded cancellation orders.

The pilot performance was at the Marriott Marquis Hotel in New York City for the International Development Research Council (IRDC), a real-estate trade group. The first full production was performed at the National Speakers Association annual convention in Washington, DC. In both cases, the scripts were rewritten to address the needs and issues of the audience.

The template production is not limited to salespeople. It's designed to be rewritten for basically any audience. Of course, there needs to be enough lead time to research and write a script. Then the cast has to learn a new script each time, even though the

blocking and choreography will mostly be the same for each show. One interesting point is that the cast members often have no idea why a certain line is funny to the audience. I tell them where to anticipate a laugh or applause, so they can pause accordingly.

To pursue this kind of production for your event, be sure to look for very talented people who can deliver the final value

for you. First find a writer who is not only funny but understands business. You want someone who can research your business to the point of being an expert. Then he or she will be ready to put it on paper for you. Try not to limit this person's creativity. If

you want a show, but it doesn't matter which music you use, let the writer choose, basing his decision on the audience. If you choose the music (unless there's a strategic reason it needs to something specific), your writer may not be able to give you the best results.

A good director is also important, especially one with "industrial" experience. The staging at most conventions has to be set up specifically for that event, so the production is often not working with the standard stage. The show has to be adapted to work within the restrictions of that stage, or, if possible, when the staging is being designed, to allow elements that would make for a smooth production. The same goes for the lighting and the sound. The sound is very important and seems to be the one area that groups scrimp on. The entire show is based on the audience hearing the lyrics. Actors can wear wireless microphones with headsets, like they do on Broadway. But it's super important to make sure that you get a crisp, clear sound from those microphones or the show will be lost.

ENDNOTES

1 "The Harder Hard Sell," *The Economist*, June 24, 2004.

2 The State of the News Media 2004. An Annual Report on American Journalism.

3 ROMI is the registered trademark of AIMS Worldwide, Inc. It's used with permission.

4 "TV ads less effective," survey, Association of National Advertisers and Forrester Research, March 26, 2006.

5 "Broadcast Engineering, Cable rates climb as broadcast TV viewership continues decline," survey, Association of National Advertisers and Forrester Research, Feb. 2, 2004.

6 "Decline in Radio Audience, Due to MP3 Players," www.anythingbutipod.com/archives/2005.

7 "Households Diary Study Shows Mail Trends," U.S. Postal Service study, POSTCOM BULLETIN 42–05, October 21, 2005, http://www.upu.int/direct_mail/en/dmab_news_2005–10_annex-01_en.pdf.

8 Denise Osburn and Dawn Kopecki, "A Way to Stretch Ad Dollars—Advertising-Cost Rebates," *Nation's Business* (May 1994); includes list of information sources.

9 Diane Brady, with David Kiley and bureau reports, "Making Marketing Measure Up; The Pressure Is On to Take the Guesswork Out of Ad Spending," *BusinessWeek Online*, December 13, 2004.

10 2002, RPI Press, ISBN 0–9718598–1–7.

11 Established in the 1970s, the former Spot Quotations and Data, Inc., legally changed its name to the acronym, SQAD, in 2001.

12 Designated Market Area (DMA) is the term used by A. C. Nielsen to describe a television view area. Area of Dominant Influence (ADI) is the term used by Arbitron to describe the same.

13 Neighborhood Marketing Tactics: Use your creativity and marketing smarts to attract loyal following of local businesspeople and residents. Entrepreneur.com, January 11, 2005.

14 This information is based upon the 1990 United States Census.

15 With permission. US Hole In One. www.HoleInOne.com, 888-882-5440.

16 Media Market Matters: As Old As Outdoor Advertising, May 15, 2006.

17 "Ethical Considerations, for the Conservation of Circus Posters," *WAAC Newsletter,* vol. 17, no. 12 (May 1995).

18 One rating point equals 1 percent of the market's population.

19 Excerpted with permission from Larry Winget. www.larrywinget .com. The Pitbull of Personal Development, Author, #1 Bestseller, *Shut Up, Stop Whining & Get A Life!* Host of the A&E television series *Big Spender.*

20 Joanne Kaufman, "How to Succeed In Business Musicals," *Wall Street Journal,* July 21, 2006.

ACKNOWLEDGMENTS

A special thanks to all those who gave advice and support: Marc Slutsky, Brad Baker, Jeff Herman, Fred Hills, Art Stevens, Joe Vincent, David Woodcock, Jeannie Sabol, Jason Harris, Scribendi, Cindy Kubica, Farris Poole, Judy Cayen, Rayad Moore, Robert L. Shook, Silvan Krel, Howard and Sonia Eichenwald. A special thanks to my daughter Amanda and my son Mitchell for their patience and understanding—yeah, right.

ABOUT THE AUTHOR

JEFF SLUTSKY is the president and CEO of Street Fighter Marketing in Columbus, Ohio. He started the company in 1980 and, along with his brother Marc, has consulted for hundreds of businesses, large and small. He has become a much-sought-after keynote speaker, corporate parody writer/producer, and seminar leader. A sampling of the companies that have worked with Jeff includes McDonald's, Subway, Molson, Chevron, the U.S. Postal Service, Goodyear, the U.S. Army, American Express, AT&T, State Farm Insurance, National City Bank, Sony, Honda, Bristol-Myers Squibb, Marvel Entertainment, and KNBC. Jeff is married and has six children, including triplets.